Golden Years

of

BURNLEY

TRUE NORTH BOOKS
DEAN CLOUGH
HALIFAX
WEST YORKS
HX3 5AX
TEL. 01422 344344
WWW.NOSTALGIA-BOOKS.CO.UK

First published in Great Britain by:
True North Books, Dean Clough, Halifax HX3 5AX
1998

ISBN 1 900 463 67 9

© Copyright: True North Books

Golden Years of Burnley

Text   Peter Thomas
Text pages design   Mandy Walker
Photographs compiled by   Phil Holland
Cover design   Mark Smith

Contents

Acknowledgments

The publishers would like to thank

Morris Bray

Reference Section - Burnley Central Library

Burnley Express

Jean Siddall

A view of Manchester Road, taken in 1950.

Introduction

Producing another book of nostalgic reflections on the Burnley we used to know was a challenge taken up enthusiastically by everyone involved.   Where possible we have tried to concentrate upon a period within the memory of most of our readers; the 1940s, 50s and 60s - decades which saw tremendous changes in the town, and a time when changes in the world of work, entertainment, public health and retailing. *Change* takes place constantly in every town and Burnley is no exception.

As we all get older it is often easier to 'step back' and view events and developments with a clearer sense of perspective. Our aim has been to assist in this respect by presenting a 'catalyst' capable of rekindling memories of days gone by in an entertaining manner. Looking through the pages of this book it may be surprising how much change has taken place, and over such a relatively short period, relative to the long history of the area. Street scenes are not neglected. Photographs of this nature were popular in the last book, and understandably so. The changing face of the town is reflected in the way our roads and shops have developed to meet the changing needs of our lives over the years. These photographs show the shops and motorcars we remember from our early days, along with the fashions which were all the rage when we were younger. All combine to refresh our memories of days gone by, and when that occurs the book will have achieved its aim.

Events and Occasions

Below: In a setting more accustomed to hearing the roar of a football crowd, Winston Churchill speaks at the microphone at Turf Moor in June 1945. This was a political rally in the lead up to the 1945 general election and the Prime Minister was speaking on behalf of the National Liberal candidate, Major HHM Mimes, who is next to Churchill in the car. Also in the photograph are the National Conservative candidates Richard Fort, standing for Clitheroe and Lt Harvey Nicholls, standing for Nelson and Colne. The war with Germany had ended in April and although the war with Japan was to continue until August, it was clear that it was now the shape of the post-war world that was uppermost in people's minds. Churchill was a great war leader and this was recognised by the people of Burnley, who gave him a hero's welcome. He was also an orator of the 'old school', at a time when public speaking was recognised as a powerful political weapon. However, the people of Burnley preferred Labour's post-war plans and in the election later that year, the Labour sitting member, Mr W A Burke was returned. This was reflected in the country at large and to the astonishment of those not familiar with democracy in the world, the great wartime leader, Churchill, was replaced by Clement Atlee. Winston looks very much at home with the microphone. One wonders what he would think of the modern political media circus, dominated by 'image' and slick television presentation.

Right: A familiar figure pauses on the steps of the Savoy in February 1927. There is already something of the 'bulldog' look about Winston Churchill, a look of stubbornness and determination which would become so famous in the war years. However, on this occasion he was visiting Burnley in his capacity as Chancellor of the Exchequer. The Burnley Conservative and Unionist Party was delighted to have such a distinguished figure come in support of its prospective parliamentary candidate, Mr Fairbairn, who can be seen on the far right of the photograph. Mr Churchill is flanked by party agent, Mr Braddock, to the left and Mr S Finburgh MP, to the right. After lunch at the Savoy Cafe, the party made its way to the Palace Theatre for a public meeting at which Churchill was the main speaker. He received a rapturous reception from Conservative supporters in the main body of the theatre, but the general public had been admitted to the gallery and he was not to get it all his own way. When he alluded to the General Strike of 1926 as, 'a conspiracy against the Commonwealth and the State', there were shouts of dissent from the gallery. There were plenty of miners in Burnley who had bitter memories of a dispute which, for them, had lasted seven months and had ended in defeat. Churchill had played a major part in this. The interruptions continued, but Winston was an old political campaigner. At the end of his speech he claimed that this was democracy in action and thanked his gallery opponents for their 'courteous behaviour'.

Burnley Express

It was, 'Hats off for their majesties', for the soldiers of the 103rd Field Brigade and the East Lancashire Regiment. The occasion was the visit to Burnley of King George VI and Queen Elizabeth on May 17th 1938. The focal point of the visit was Bank Hall Hospital and the factory of Platers and Stampers. The King and Queen are pictured descending the steps of the dais that had been erected in the forecourt of the factory, followed by the Mayor and Mayoress. The visit was part of a tour of Lancashire and the royal car passed through Brierfield on its way from Nelson. The mills of Brierfield closed for an hour and schoolchildren helped to swell the throngs lining the royal route. Hawkers apparently did a good trade, selling miniature flags, button-holes, ribbons etc. Around the area of the dais, people had been gathering since early morning. Some of them risked life and limb to scramble onto walls and roofs for vantage points. The Royal couple arrived at 11am and met civic dignitaries, along with representatives of organisations such as the Scouts, the Guides and the Police. Some disabled ex-servicemen were presented and 150 selected school-children had grandstand seats for the visit - an exciting day for those lucky ones. This was a day to savour for Burnley, for there had been nothing similar since 1913 and the visit of George V and Queen Mary. The next royal occasion would not be too far distant, but not before the dark days of World War Two had intervened.

Burnley Express

Burnley Express

Above: Public and private buildings throughout Burnley did their best to celebrate in style the Coronation of King George VI in 1937. The Tram Office in St James's Street was no exception and whoever was in charge had made a thorough job of draping the building in a colourful and patriotic way. Bunting, flags and streamers can be seen in abundance. Someone with an artistic eye had adapted the red, white and blue chains to the shape of the building so that the apex, the large crown, was situated at the apex of the frontage. Just as eye catching are the portraits in the centre, those of the king and queen, flanked by the young princesses. Elizabeth is to the left and Margaret to the right. The inscription below is plain enough and above it was made clear that this token of loyalty was the work of Burnley, Colne and Nelson Joint Transport. This body had enjoyed control

of local passenger transport from 1933 and in fact trams had stopped running in 1935 due to the increasing use and popularity of motor buses, which had been introduced in 1924. Thus had ended a history of tram transport in Burnley which had begun with steam trams in 1883. The people of Burnley were probably glad to 'let their hair down' and rejoice a little bit in 1937 and again the following year to celebrate a royal visit. Events on the European scene were taking a sombre turn, with Hitler showing increasing aggression and it was clear to many that another war might well be looming up.

Top: The Town Hall clock approaches midday on May 12th 1937 and plenty of patriotic sentiment is on display as the building stands impressively decorated for the coronation of King George VI. The Union Flag is much in evidence, as is the Cross of St George. The new king had been unexpectedly propelled into the position of monarch by the abdication of his older brother, Edward VIII in 1936. Older readers will no doubt remember the whole abdication crisis, beginning with the king's entanglement with the American divorcee, Mrs Wallis Simpson and ending with the radio broadcast in which he announced that he was forsaking the throne for the woman he loved. The shock waves did not shake the fundamental loyalty of people towards the monarchy in those days and the banners proclaiming 'God Save The King' and 'God Save Our King And Queen', were real expressions of the feelings of the majority of the populace. Hanging over the entrance to the Town Hall are cameo portraits of the new king and queen, who were to visit Burnley the following year. Of course Burnley did not simply mark the 1937 Coronation with a decorative Town Hall and the right-hand poster of the three on the railing concerns 'Coronation Celebrations', including 'Sports'. No doubt the youngsters thoroughly enjoyed themselves, oblivious of the solemn events of 1936 which had brought them their extra treats.

Burnley Express

The usual array of heroes, villains, dancing maidens and those who clump about behind stage, is represented in this wonderful old photograph of the cast of 'The Slave of Araby', presented by Brunswick Methodist Church, around 1930. Some of our older readers might recognise themselves and certainly many others might pick out mothers, fathers, aunts, uncles or grandparents. There are a couple of villainous looking characters on the left and surely the hero of the piece is the strong and dependable looking gentleman, front row, second from the right. The costumes look magnificent, but make no mistake, it is a real vicar on the front row, the Reverend C B Johnson. To the immediate left of him is, possibly, the heroine of the story. The whole scene is hugely nostalgic of a time that was pre-television, pre-video and pre-computer. There was entertainment to be had at the cinema and theatre, but most pleasure of all was derived from the 'do-it-yourself' brand. Almost every church and chapel, particularly through their Sunday Schools, was able to put on some sort of show every year. At Christmas, there was usually some local choral society presenting the 'Messiah'. Such community spirit and what a host of happy memories must lie locked in that picture. One curious point, however. Then, as now, amateur operatic societies seemed to have struggled to get enough men in their casts. Attractive young females dominate our photograph. Of the men featured, two were scenery painters and one was the accompanist! The devastating effects of World War One could partly have accounted for this in 1930, but not today. Try your hand at assessing the male to female ratio at the next amateur show you attend, unless its 'Ali Baba and the Forty Thieves' of course!

Burnley Express

In the Spring of 1945 the end of the Second World War was in sight, but anxiety for those Burnley people who had loved ones fighting abroad must have been no less. In addition the country had endured a gruelling 41/2 years with shortages and restrictions. Such simple, everyday items as bananas and oranges had become a rarity. In this atmosphere of austerity, the royal visit of King George VI and Queen Elizabeth to Burnley, on March 8th 1945, must have done something to lighten the gloom.

Although this was an 'Eve of Victory' tour, the need for security meant that there was no public announcement of the visit. However, the decorations being hastily erected at public buildings first thing in the morning soon alerted the Burnley public and as it usually does, news spread fast. Huge crowds, hastily released from schools, shops and factories, poured onto the streets and the photograph of the royal cavalcade coming down Manchester Road towards the Town Hall conveys the excitement of it all. This was

shortly after 10am and the pavements were packed with cheering onlookers. Those who had managed to scramble onto the wall top, to the right, gained an excellent view of the gleaming vehicles.

A short reception was held at the Town Hall where the royal couple met civic leaders, but also people who represented different facets of Burnley life. They spoke to veterans of the cotton and mining industries. Also, serving as a reminder that the war was not yet quite over, they were introduced to Private R L Rockliffe, who had lost an arm at Arnhem. Shortly before leaving, both the King and the Queen signed the Town Hall Visitors' Book. The picture shows King George VI, in RAF uniform and watching with interest is the Mayor, Alderman T P Taylor. The brief visit ended with the car cavalcade proceeding along Manchester Road, St James's Street, Westgate and Accrington Road. Then it was back to work for the people of Burnley, albeit with spirits uplifted by this unifying occasion.

Burnley Express

©Burnley Express

The crowning of a young queen at the Coronation of 1953 seemed to mark a turning point in the life of Britain. The new Elizabethan Age had dawned and with it the end of the austerity of the immediate post-war years. People seemed able, at last, to shrug off the legacy of the war years and look to the future. Better times lay ahead. The 'Elizabethan Serenade' was composed; a new magazine, the 'Young Elizabethan', was published; both symbols of the new era. It was in this atmosphere of optimism that Queen Elizabeth II and HRH Duke of Edinburgh visited Burnley on April 14th 1955. The procession route was packed as the people of Burnley turned out in unprecedented numbers. The buildings were awash with colour as flags and bunting were hung and draped everywhere. Upstairs windows were crammed with those lucky enough to secure a grand-stand view. Excitement built up as the hour approached and those in the vicinity of the Town Hall were well enter-tained as the band of the 1st Battalion, the Loyal Regiment, played selections. Soldiers lined the streets and some of the East Lancashire Regiment, along with 'B' Battalion of the Home Guard, assisted the police guard. At last the moment arrived and the lines of soldiers smartly 'presented arms' as, at 1.30pm, the motorcade swept down Manchester Road. The reception was overwhelming - cheering, shouting, clapping, flag-waving - and this reached a crescendo as the royal couple stepped out of their gleaming limousine at the Town Hall. Here they were greeted by the Mayor and Mayoress, Alderman Joseph and Mrs Herbert. A special platform and canopy had been built at the Town Hall entrance, with red carpeted steps and alongside the platform was a stand to accommodate 300 VIPs and representatives of community organisations. As the Queen and the Duke reached the platform, they turned to wave at the crowds, who now had the opportunity to see that she was wearing a grey-blue fitted coat, with matching petal hat. She also wore a triple row of pearls and carried a diamond brooch in her lapel. High above the crowds, two aeroplane wove vapour trails in the shape of 'ER' in the sky. The royal party had lunch at the Town Hall, after having waved to the crowd from the balcony. The Queen was very much impressed by the bank of spring flowers which seemed to cascade down the walls. She also commented on the luncheon table floral display, which had been arranged by Mrs Robinson of the Moorcock Inn, Waddington. After lunch, the Queen said to the Mayor 'We have had a most enjoyable stay ... You have enter-tained us wonderfully well'. Before departure, both the Queen and the Duke signed the Visitors' Book and their portraits. Later that day 5000 people would come to look, paying 6d each into the Mayor's Fund for the Elderly.

Continued overleaf

Burnley Express

The royal couple stepped out into the spring sunshine at 2.45pm, to be greeted by yet another wall of sound from the crowds. About 20,000 people had packed the centre of Burnley, some even having found their way onto the roofs. From the Town Hall, the motorcade went down Manchester Road and along St James's Street. Amongst a party of 400 elderly people seated outside the Empress Ballroom was 88 year old Mrs Esther Brophy, who had once seen the Queen's great, great grandmother, Queen Victoria, at St Helens. The bells of St Peter's Parish Church were ringing and at this point hundreds of excited children had been assembled to add their voices to the waves of noise. The royal cars then moved along Colne Road, to be greeted by nurses and miners in the Bank Hall area and on through Brierfield. The excitement was over for Burnley but was just beginning for Nelson and Colne, where the visit continued. Queen Elizabeth's train was pulled out of Colne station, at the conclusion of the visit, by two 'Jubilee' Class engines, 'India' and 'South Africa', an echo of an historic, Imperial past.

The year of the Coronation of Queen Elizabeth II, 1953, was a landmark. Ration books might still linger on from the war years, but now was the time to look forward to progress and prosperity - the new Elizabethan Age. It is easy to forget how, in the 1950s, unswerving loyalty to the crown was widespread. There was very little cynicism. The National Anthem was always played at the end of public performances and almost everyone stood respectfully throughout, some at attention. Therefore, June 2nd 1953 found Burnley, in common with the rest of Britain, ready to celebrate. Public and private buildings had been patriotically decorated, although the weather hardly did justice to the occasion. It was cold and dull throughout, with squally showers of rain from time to time. This was not quite yet the television age. Few people owned one and so it was a matter of friends gathering wherever a television was available to watch the ceremony at Westminster Abbey, in 'glorious black and white' of course. Then, in the afternoon it was party time.

The people of Burnley were determined to enjoy themselves come what may. There were literally scores of street parties, reflecting community spirit as well as patriotism, although the weather forced some to adapt to indoor versions. The one at Swainbank Street was held in a garage and was organised by Mrs Kenneford and Mrs Giles. Thirty children were each given a Coronation mug, filled with sweets and a gift. They are seen here pausing long enough for a photograph to be taken before falling on the tempting plates of cakes and buns in front of them. There are plenty of cheerful faces and an interesting selection of hats. The number of outdoor coats really does give some idea of the chilliness of the day, but spirits were not dampened. Plenty of the distinctive Coronation mugs are on view, but it is a fair guess that not many have survived until the present day.

The residents of Snowden Street chose a garden effect for their outside decorations, but for food and celebrations they joined the people of Cumberland Avenue in Rosegrove Methodist School. A number of the children pictured have turned the event into a fancy-dress one, including the two 'Welsh girls' at the back. Smiling faces, young and old, beam at the camera, but what a shame that one youngster at the front has lost his or her moment of glory by deciding, at this precise moment, to do some shoe adjustments. One row back and in the middle, we have what must be our local Coronation Queen, surrounded by her retinue. However, the number of 'pinnies' on view is a reminder that, whatever the occasion, somebody has to do the washing up. Nobody was forgotten at this Rosegrove celebration, for after tea the children were given gifts and the elderly received parcels.

Coronation Day 1953 was not allowed to fade away quietly in Burnley. A newsreel of the ceremony had been rushed northwards and was screened that very evening at the Odeon. Also a Civic Ball was held at the Mechanics' Institute, with music relayed out to Manchester Road to allow dancing in the street.

This photograph is undated, but it has a look of the fifties about it. What a charming sight as the young children of Sion Baptist Church lead the procession. The Primary Division is in the vanguard, followed further down St James's Street by the Junior Division. Young girls dominate the foreground and how splendid they look with their long dresses and bouquets. How they must have looked forward to this day and a chance to dress as princesses. It is not clear what occasion this was, but certainly church and chapel processions, to celebrate anniversaries or national events, go back well into the nineteenth century. Whitsun Walks, for example, were a very popular feature up to the First World War, but the advent of the charabanc tended to turn these into Whitsun outings. Whatever the occasion, it appears to have been a fine day, attracting huge crowds. An examination of the ladies lining the pavements will show that it was definitely a 'best hats' day. Also, judging from the direction in which the people further down the street are gazing, there is more to come, possibly marchers from other churches. The distinctive white facings of the Burton building show very prominently in the background and if any reader wants to put a precise date on the photograph, there may be a clue on the right. The Palace Theatre is featuring the film 'Darby O'Gill and the Little People' and this provided a role for none other than Sean Connery.

Left: In the 1890s Robert Halstead, the mill-working visionary who lived not too far from Burnley, insisted that as well as political advancement, ordinary people should be seeking to conquer 'the kingdom of the mind', ie knowledge.

To this end, he organised a series of lectures by Oxford professors to local Workers' Educational Associations. The Burnley Central Library has always had much the same attitude towards widening the horizons of the young people of the district and it was in this spirit that the 'Focus on Youth' lectures were launched in the 1940s. The speaker on October 21st 1949 was Captain C W R Knight and the title of his lecture was 'Adventures with Eagles'. Here we can see him, on the steps of the library, with a magnificent, but rather fearsome eagle on his arm. The enthralled children are gathered in a group around the eagle, whose name was Mr Ramshaw and their expressions range from delight to apprehension.

The little boy on the left is interested enough, but he is staying well out of range of that beak. This series of lectures ran until February 1950 and the theme of adventure in the wider world was reflected in such titles as 'Scott's Last Expedition' and 'Lapland'.

The age of television had brought adventure into the living room by the 1960s, but even so a similar series of lectures for young people was presented between 1967 and 1968, including 'Fifteen Months in a Volcanic Paradise' and 'A Journey to India'.

Above: A stirring sight of military precision is on view marching along St James's Street in June 1953. No sooner had the pageantry of the Coronation passed, with the decorations still evident on the buildings, than the people of Burnley were treated to another colourful spectacle as the East Lancashire Regiment received the freedom of the borough. The ceremony took place at the Town Hall and the Colonel of the Regiment, Brigadier J W Pendlebury, DSO, MC, spoke of the close links between the regiment and Burnley. The town had been the traditional home of the regiment, with a barracks there and Burnley itself was the largest recruiting area. As the regimental colours and the Queen's colours were unfurled, for the first time ever in a Burnley parade, the Scroll of Freedom was presented by the Mayor, Alderman H Hudson. This entitled the 'East Lancs' to march through Burnley with colours flying, drums beating, bands playing and bayonets fixed. Unlike Coronation Day, the weather was good and Burnley people were treated to not just one parade, but two. The regiment marched from the Artillery Barracks and ex-servicemen of the regiment marched from the Drill Hall. The band of the First Battalion, magnificent in blue and scarlet, had returned from Suez specially for this occasion. Local connections were well represented in the band. Sixteen year old Lance Corporal Stan Clewlow, of Clegg Street, was playing a cornet and other locals were J Jewell of Brierfield and Joe Murtagh of Higher Brunshaw. A marching band is irresistible to small boys and the photograph reveals one trying to get in on the act.

*The Mayoral procession of the
1961 Centenary celebrations*

Centenary Way is Burnley's physical landmark to commemorate the fact that 1961 marked the 100th Anniversary of the granting of Burnley's Charter, by which the town gained a greater degree of independence and self-control in 1861. One hundred years later, the town prepared to celebrate in style and there were more reasons than one for rejoicing. With Burnley FC a major force in British and European football and acting as an ambassador for the town, along with the publicity from the locally shot film, 'Whistle Down the Wind', the early 1960s was a time of optimism and confidence for Burnley. Therefore the Centenary Carnival of 1961 was a celebration of all the factors that stirred pride in the hearts of Burnley folk.

June 24th 1961 was a bright and sunny day, one which fitted the occasion. The Carnival began with a three and a half mile long procession which snaked its way through the town centre. This commenced at 1.30pm and it was thanks to the organisation of the Marshal, Mr Herbert Wilkinson and his team of assistants, that everything proceeded so smoothly. The police too played their part as the Carnival procession took two hours to move through Burnley. The Band and Drums of the Lancashire Regiment provided a musical vanguard, slightly upstaged by the prancing character of 'Waltzing Matilda' who, at one point, placed himself at the very head of the procession. Hardly had the crowd got over the expertise of the drum major hurling his baton into the air, than it was able to admire the Mayor's car. For this auspicious occasion the Mayor, Alderman E Sandy and his Lady Mayoress, were carried in a superb open-topped Chevrolet Belair. A more modest fleet of cars followed, although the third one, with the Carnival Queen on board, was a sporty little Renault Florida.

Burnley Girls' High School providing a spectacle

Burnley Express

Jackson's Milk contribution to the celebrations.

Burnley, Colne & Nelson Joint Transport

Burnley Express

The floats that then followed gave the large and appreciative crowd which lined the streets some idea of the wholehearted effort that had gone in to make this such a memorable day. Hundreds of people and dozens of organisations had laboured for long hours to ensure that this was going to be the best procession ever seen in Burnley. The colourful spectacle, with its sheer inventiveness, drew gasps and applause along the route. The floats featured in these photographs are just a few of the many outstanding creations witnessed that day. Burnley Girls' High School displayed different styles of dress as between 1861 and 1961 in various areas of life, eg the schoolroom, tennis, cycling. The impressive old 'boneshaker' bicycle was perhaps the star of the show. The theme of Burnley Grammar School was that of 400 years of academic excellence in buildings old and new. The more formal 'cap and gown' era was featured on the right, with the more informal laboratory research on the left. The decorated bus of Burnley, Colne and Nelson Joint Transport was a startling affair. The 'Travel by Bus' theme on the side suggested some of the attractions that were only a bus ride away - Turf Moor, Thompson Park, Towneley Hall etc. The front proudly bore the Corporation Arms, with pictures of older forms of Burnley road transport. Hundreds of bulbs ensured that this would be an even more spectacular display by night. The GPO float contrasted the 1911 switch-board girls with their 1961 counterparts and the national dress on display highlighted the inter-national communications revolution. The making of 'bonny babies' by Jackson's Milk obviously met the approval of the cheerful crowd behind the vintage milk cart.

The Carnival procession eventually wound its way to Prairie Field. At the Mayor's Marquee, Alderman Sandy said, 'I cannot remember anything else better in its way in the past half-century'. The cheers from the crowd suggested that he was not alone in this opinion. Even in the best organised events, however, things can go wrong. Two parachutists from the Special Air Service jumped from 30,000 feet with the intention of landing in a marked and prepared area on the Carnival ground. Unfortunately, cross winds blew them across Colne Road and into fields beyond. So much was happening that day that passing motorists probably thought that it was all carefully planned and part of the show. The Centenary celebrations carried on regardless at Prairie Field, and elsewhere, to provide a memorable day for the people of Burnley.

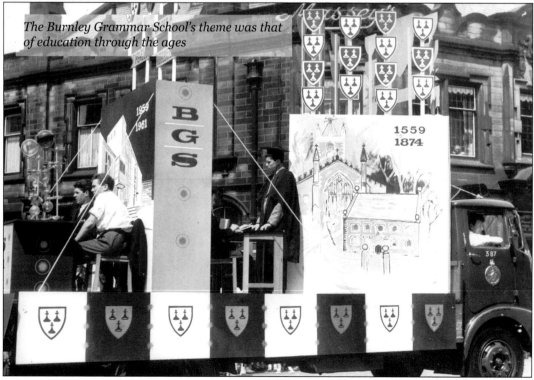

The Burnley Grammar School's theme was that of education through the ages

The GPO float contrasted the 1911 switchboard girls with their 1961 counterparts

Burnley Express

Above: Another photograph in this book features the Safety First Bus, aimed principally at getting a message across to children. The stark message of 'Don't Gamble With Death' on this photograph, is aimed fairly and squarely at drivers. This is reinforced by the mutilated car atop the Leyland truck. Careful examination of the gambler's dice reveal two of the culprits thought responsible for road accidents - 'alcohol' and 'speeding'. It is a matter for speculation as to what factors the other dice blamed. The location appears to be the Perseverance Mills, according to the faint sign on the wall behind. As the truck belongs to British Road Services, the nationalised arm of road transport, this brings this scene at least into the 1950s and it was probably part of a government campaign. The growth of car ownership since the Second World War has opened new worlds to very many people, but one of the downsides has been the growing death toll on the roads. The Safety Truck featured in the photograph was impressive publicity for its day and some readers may remember it, but the government has increasingly turned to television as the most powerful medium for the road safety message. There is evidence to show that the roads are a safer place, in proportion to the volume of traffic, than they used to be, but is this due to persuasion or compulsion? Our shattered car on the back of the truck pre-dates the breathaliser, the MOT and seat belts. Much as we grumble about restrictions, do we really want to rattle around in our badly maintained cars, stopping at every public house for a drink? Count to ten before you answer.

Below: This Safety First Bus was an imaginative attempt by Burnley, Colne and Nelson Joint Transport to grab attention during its Children's Safety Week. The date is unknown, but the problem is perennial - how to train children to be aware of the dangers of traffic and how to make drivers pay more attention to the presence and possible unpredictability of children. The message to drivers on the side of the bus is simple enough, that 'children should be seen and not hurt', a variation on an old saying. The tiger leaping from the bus is a message to children of the danger that can lurk in something as commonplace as a bus. The reverse of the bus, which cannot be seen in this picture, is aimed at both parents and children, stressing the old Kerb Drill and urging parents to teach children to use the beacon controlled crossings. Perhaps some readers experienced the Safety Bus at first hand, but for most of us our memories probably picture a friendly constable visiting school, armed with his portable belisha beacons etc. The old Kerb Drill of, 'Look right; look left; and then look right again', will be instinctive among older readers. Younger ones will remember the concentration on zebra crossings and the injunction to, 'Stop, Look and Listen', as well as the famous Green Cross Code. The Tufty Club is still going strong in schools. Whatever the approach, teaching road safety to children continues to be vital. But for this campaigning, those terrible figures on the Safety Bus would have worsened rather than improved in proportion to the growth of traffic.

The Centenary Carnival of 1961, to mark the 100th Anniversary of Burnley's attainment of chartered borough status, will have left a variety of memories for Burnley people. It might be the memory of decorating a float; or the excitement of riding on a float, in fancy dress, through the cheering crowds; or it might simply be the fond recollection of watching the whole colourful pageant. For those who competed for the title of Centenary Queen, the dominant memory might be that of a nerve-racking occasion, or just a bit of fun. The winner was Jacqueline Woodruff and this charming picture shows her enthroned with her handsome trophy, her sash and a bouquet. The idea of crowning a young lady as 'Queen' of some festival or event goes back as far as the beginning of recorded history. From the local May Queens and Sunday School Anniversary Queens, with their roots in the past, we can go across the spectrum to the hype and 'razzmatazz' of the modern Miss World contests. Carnival Queens, of course, are expected to spend the year of their office attending various events and looking constantly radiant. The glamour of the position must wear a bit thin on an open platform in the driving rain. Still-smile- that is what you have to do. Jacqueline's first duty was to ride in an open-topped Renault Florida in the Carnival Procession, which must have been thrilling. She was also in the position of knowing that her title was unique to her. There can never be another Burnley Centenary Queen.

Burnley Express

Above: Warwick Street celebrations were in full flow when this picture was taken as Burnley rejoiced at the coronation of the new Queen. It was June 1953 and it seemed as if the whole town was in party mood, such was the extent of the loyalty felt for the youthful Queen Elizabeth. The residents had put on a fine spread for the children of the street. No doubt a memory or two of the V.E and V.J celebrations held around eight years earlier would have been jogged by the occasion. The pavement glistens after a light shower which had threatened to spoil the day. Indeed, we know from accounts from the time that the decision was taken was taken later to move the celebrations inside. Keen eyes may be able to make out the royal crest on some of the mugs in the picture. These had been thoughtfully distributed to local children, full of chocolates and toffees and three shiny shilling pieces. It is said that there was dancing in the streets to the sound of 'amplified music' for the adults and a heartfelt vote of thanks to Ann Shaw, Peter Murgatroyd, Tony Newton, Linda Hillen and Kathleen Sagar for organising the party.

Right: The 1961 celebrations of the centenary of Burnley's gaining of borough status, coincided with the fiftieth anniversary of the Burnley Scouting Association and so there was a double reason for holding a scout jamboree. This was held at Prairie Field, on the weekend of July 28th to July 30th 1961 and was attended by 280 scouts from 14 local troops. Scouts of all ages are seen around the Mayor, Councillor E Sandy, who was a visitor to the camp that weekend, along with his wife, the Mayoress. They are a well turned out squad, with lots of badges and stripes showing and no doubt the fresh air and exercise gave them all a healthy appetite. If that is one of the camp cooks, wearing an apron on the right, he was no doubt kept busy.

The scouts' uniforms are familiar enough today, but older ex-scouts may remember Baden Powell style hats; a knife clipped to the belt with a spike for getting stones out of horses' hoofs - alas, rarely used. And last, but not least, the staff that a scout often carried around in his hand, for no known reason. Did the word 'woggle' carry as much amusement in 1961 as it used to do? For the weekend jamboree of 1961, there was a sports day on the Saturday and a camp competition.

The photograph shows proud award winners. Over 1,000 visitors came along and no doubt quite a few made a good job of tripping over the guy ropes of the tents in the rear.

Burnley Express

Left: Hayley Mills, famous daughter of a famous father, is seen at the centre of this photograph, arriving with her mother for the premiere of the film, 'Whistle Down the Wind', at the Odeon in 1961. Famous figures in the film industry, Richard Attenborough and Bryan Forbes, were producer and director of the film. Hayley was the juvenile star in an interesting and unusual film about a group of children who, stumbling upon a bearded tramp in a barn, come to believe that he is Jesus. Burnley and its surrounding area was the location and local children appeared in the film. Diane Holgate, then aged ten and Alan Barnes aged eight, from the village of Chatburn, came across on the screen as 'naturals'. Before the premiere at the Odeon, there was a reception at the Keirby and one feature of this was a chocolate and sugar model of a scene from the film. As Hayley arrived at the Odeon, she was presented with a pair of clogs by her understudy, Christine Ashworth of Padiham. Apparently Hayley had expressed an interest in buying a pair. The picture shows this little presentation and gives some idea of the crowds attracted to this 'glitzy'

event. The St John's Ambulance volunteers are lined up, ready to do their usual sterling work. Along with 'Whistle Down the Wind', the audience was treated to a film about Burnley FC who, along with Spurs, dominated English football at this time. These were heady days for Burnley.

Below: This magnificent group photograph was taken to show how the residents of Springfield Road celebrated the coronation of Queen Elizabeth II. A wonderful cake in the shape of a crown was baked and iced by former army catering instructor J. Riley and it is shown here in the centre of the picture surrounded by admiring children. The picture was taken in June 1953 making most of the children mature 50 *somethings* at the time of writing. It is clear that something amusing had been said judging by the smiles on some of the youngsters in the group. They all look delightful and well-turned out for the day. The residents in the area organised races and other events to keep the children amused through the day, topped off with an impressive fireworks display in the evening.

Burnley Express

Twenty-five years on from the accession of Queen Elizabeth II in 1952 and it was time for more royal celebrations in Burnley with the Silver Jubilee. How the world had changed since 1952 - the Beatles, space travel, colour television - and so much more. Two things remained little different from the Coronation celebrations of 1953 - the weather and Burnley's enthusiasm. It was yet again cold and damp in early June 1977, but once again this did not deter the citizens of Burnley from getting out and having street parties.

A prize party indeed took place at Milan Avenue, where the cheerful children are pictured at a table that is positively 'groaning' with goodies. It appears as if everyone is having a good time, with the possible exception of the rather forlorn looking dog, which looks to have turned its back in disgust. There was good reason for the party spirit, for the Milan Avenue 'Pirates' had just won First Prize in the 'Burnley Express' street party contest. At the far end of the table, proudly displaying the prize of 72 cans of ale can be seen three of the happy organisers. These were, from left to right, Mrs Joan Wareing, Mrs Doreen Pye and Mrs Barbara Broxton. By the time the cans were empty, no doubt they were happier still! Milan Street's award was the result of a combined effort, but the judges had been really impressed by Mrs Evelyn Riddle's eight foot high paintings of scarlet-uniformed guardsmen. However, the children had also contributed by drawing Micky Mouse cartoons and a

Jubilee Queen had been elected, 18 year old Kathryn Bond. In the 'Burnley Express' competition, Second Prize went to Gainsborough Avenue and Dall Street gained Third Prize. The latter is featured in the second photograph, and the scene is typical of many from that Jubilee weekend. An ambitious decorative scheme is the main feature, with a large Union Jack as the centrepiece. It must have taken a real co-operative effort to get that flag and the bunting in place and this happy picture shows a real community spirit. It's thumbs up for the camera on the front row and cheery waves and smiles all around.

It is interesting to contrast both these 1977 Jubilee photographs with the Swainbank Street Coronation party of 1953, elsewhere in this book. We had begun to live in the 'plastic age' by 1977. The beakers on show on Milan Street contrast nicely with the mugs of Swainbank Street. More obviously, the children of 1977 were dressed much more informally than those of 1953 and had also become fashion conscious. Youngsters from ordinary households in 1953 could not afford to think about fashion, but just take a look at those 'flares' in our second 1977 street scene.

One of the larger-scale events to celebrate the Jubilee was put on by the Burnley and Calder Round Tables. There were entertainments in the Market Square and the water in the fountains miraculously turned pink. The procession to the gala at Towneley Park contained 40 floats and the Jubilee Queen was Denise Bate-Jones.

Wartime

The response from Kitchener's call was generous, but not enough to keep pace with the carnage

This immaculately dressed young lady was known as 'Young Kitchener' and she sported the correct military attire down to gloves, spurs and swagger stick. During World War One, 'Young Kitchener', alias Jennie Jackson, stood on her own special corner in Burnley, on Saturdays, collecting money for comforts for the troops. Her placard read that she was collecting for soldiers' and sailors' parcels and appealed to the public to, 'Please spare a copper'. No doubt her charming appearance touched many hearts, especially those with loved ones far away and she raised an estimated £4,000 for her worthy causes. 'Young Kitchener' is posing beside a splendid and sturdy old Vulcan ambulance. This she was well entitled to do, for apart from her other efforts, she also raised £1,000 to buy one of these vehicles for the soldiers. The date on the photograph is a poignant one, for that was the very year the real Kitchener, Minister for War, launched his famous poster recruiting campaign. This was one of the most enduring images to emerge from the Home Front - Kitchener with his handle bar moustache, fierce gaze and pointing hand. 'Your Country Needs You'. Thousands answered the recruiting call, stirred by simple patriotism, many from Burnley and the surrounding area. Our war memorials indicate how many did not return, so great was the slaughter on the Western Front, Gallipoli and elsewhere. The response to Kitchener's call was generous, but the number of volunteers could not keep pace with the carnage and by 1916 conscription had begun. An interesting footnote to the 'Young Kitchener' story is that she continued her charity work after the war, particularly for St Dunstan's, whose purpose was to help those military personnel who had been blinded during the war.

This picture represents both the best and the worst of the human spirit. These boys were Jewish refugees from Czechoslovakia in 1938, who were greatly helped to settle in Burnley by Miss Ruby McKay, headmistress of the Open-Air School. It was in 1938 that the infamous Munich Agreement was made between the British Prime Minister, Neville Chamberlain and Hitler. This handed over the Sudetenland part of Czechoslovakia to Hitler and no doubt Jewish people there feared that they would undergo the same sort of persecution that was already being suffered by German Jews, or worse. Some got away, or at least got their children away, to escape the terrible fate of those who stayed. No doubt these boys arrived in Burnley bewildered and unhappy, probably speaking little or no English. Miss McKay stood for human and Christian values, precisely opposite to those which had driven these boys from their homes. Not only was she head of the Open-Air School at Thompson Park, but she also taught as a Sunday School teacher at St Stephen's Church. She was known for her work in visiting the sick and the elderly in hospitals. Her whole life was spent in public service and to her these refugees were simply people in need of help. She responded as she always did in these circumstances and no doubt the warmth and friendliness of Burnley people made her task easier. They too had a greater understanding of right and wrong than some of the politicians of the day.

Above: This sleek line of war ambulances, photographed at the Queensgate depot during the Second World War, looks almost as if it has formed itself, without human aid. The ambulances seem to be standing to attention, ready for action. Newsreels of German Stuka dive bombing of defenceless cities in the Spanish Civil War had led the government to expect massive civilian casualties from air-raids when World War Two broke out. Not known at the time, for fear that the information would cause mass hysteria, the government itself had ordered over a million coffins to be made. Hospitals were to be made ready for a flood of victims and such places as church halls were being prepared to accommodate the overspill. It was in this sombre context that these ambulances would have been viewed at the time. The 'Blitz' did occur and many British cities took a heavy pounding, but thanks to the success of radar and British fighter aircraft, the feared casualty levels were never reached. Burnley escaped with one bomb only, but there would have been plenty of good work for these ambulances to do during a war. Lovers of old vehicles will admire them for their looks alone. The inscription on the side of the nearest ambulance reads 'Presented by Mr and Mrs Percy Thompson to the County Borough of Burnley'. There were many ways of contributing to the war effort.

Below: As war became imminent in 1939, all manner of terrifying precautions began to take place to protect the civilian population from bombing and other forms of air attack. It was feared that towns and cities would be utterly devastated, for not long before, the British Prime Minister, Baldwin, had said that, 'the bomber will always get through'. Some readers will remember Anderson and Morrison shelters, the issue of gas masks and the appearance of air-raid shelters. These squat, ugly buildings were built in school playgrounds, in factory yards and alongside terraces, like the one pictured on Thorn Street. They were dark, smelly and uncomfortable, but people were glad enough of their presence when the air-raid sirens went off in the fearful early days of the war. Plenty of German planes droned in the night skies above Burnley during the 'Blitz', but their target was usually Manchester or Liverpool. Only one bomb, a stray one, fell on Burnley and this hit Thompson Park on October 27th 1940. Undoubtedly more people in Burnley were injured by falling over in the blackout than by enemy action. Another bomb fell at Crown Point, which was a decoy airfield. Air-raid shelters lingered on for a few years after the war, becoming a dangerous sort of adventure playground for children, or a convenient place to dump unwanted rubbish. Now they have long gone and thankfully for Burnley folk, they were never really needed for their original purpose.

During the Second World War, the Home Front was regarded as vital if the war was to be won. The government employed compulsion in areas such as rationing and munitions production, but voluntary service was regarded as extremely important, for the upkeep of morale if nothing else. One of the organisations that was regarded as much more than simply a morale booster was the Home Guard. In May 1940, the government appealed to those who were not in military service to joint the Local Defence Volunteers (LDV), which was renamed the Home Guard in July 1940. They were to be part-time soldiers and at first their task was very specific - to defend strategic and vulnerable points against enemy paratroop attack.

The photograph (right) of 1941 shows 'G' Company of the 29th Battalion of the Home Guard, based at the Town Hall. In fact, the first seven Company Headquarters were all established near the Leeds and Liverpool Canal in 1940, with a view to its protection, eg Summit Company, Canal Yard, Manchester Road; Ightenhill Hill Company, Claremont School. The image of the Home Guard left to future generations is the one immortalised in the television series 'Dad's Army' and even at the time it was realised that volunteers would be able to do little against highly trained parachutists. From the very first, the initials LDV came to stand for 'Look, Duck and Vanish'. The initial problem was shortage of weapons. To drill with walking sticks was a familiar routine. Had it come to fighting, most companies would have had to rely on knives, clubs, spears and the type of home-made bomb which later became called the 'Molotov Cocktail'.

Nevertheless, the group of the Home Guard pictured overleaf, marching down Standish Street, past the Derby Arms, looks smart enough. Plenty of rifles are on display; shoes shine; and all are in step. What the photograph illustrates very well, is the age factor.

The Home Guard was usually composed of those too young for active service and those too old - 'Long Dentured Veterans' was another version of LDV. As time passed, training and equipment improved. Military ranks were introduced and it was compulsory to attend at least 48 hours training per month. Major exercises in the countryside were held.

The photograph above shows local men out on an exercise somewhere, possibly getting hot water for washing. One or two of the men are of the 'long dentured' variety, but it was in camps such as this that the Pendle Home Guard trained for its attack on Burnley, a major exercise in October 1941. The Burnley Home Guard was given the task of defending the town against attack from the men of Pendle. In the interests of realism, there was street fighting, mock explosions and imitation gas. Householders were encouraged to co-operate by looking out for saboteurs and 'fifth columnists'. One Pendle soldier was foolhardy enough to enter a Burnley house in which a blazing domestic row was at its height. He quickly surrendered when a slab of margarine, hurled at husband by wife, narrowly missed the invader's head. In spite of this, the Burnley men lost the exercise.

By 1943 any serious threat of enemy invasion had passed and active encouragement for men to join the Home Guard ceased. Attendances at parade became voluntary and by December 1945 the organisation was disbanded. The photograph of men training in Abel Street schoolyard is from 1945 and it is clearly a leadership exercise, for all the men have 'stripes up'. Their youthful appearance suggests that they may be looking to a future in the army. The Home Guard has provided a rich vein for comedy since those years and people usually like to remember the ridiculous and the absurd. However, at the time, it gave many men the feeling that they were 'doing their bit' for their country,

At leisure

Left: The four women smile briefly at the camera before continuing their vital war work. This was the busy scene at the Trafalgar Street works of Lupton and Place sometime during World War Two. Both the world wars were total wars in the sense of needing the commitment and involvement of the entire working population. There were many ways of contributing to the war effort on the Home Front, from collecting salvage to joining the Home Guard, but nothing could have been much more vital than keeping weapons and supplies flowing to the front line troops. Burnley produced munitions, parachutes and aircraft parts, among other things and as in World War One, the female population played a predominant role. This kind of work was supposed to have acted as a liberating influence in the first great conflict, but in this case Lancashire women were liberated enough, having long since established themselves in the cotton industry. However, the slump of the 1930s had reduced employment for everyone in the North and so in this sense the war provided a new opportunity for women. Money was said to be good in munitions, but by the looks of this photograph the women earned it. This appears to be the foundry floor. Clogs and long aprons are the order of the day and the women are holding some pretty 'man size' shovels. It was hard, dirty work. Still, it paid better than scrubbing the doorstep back home. Lupton and Place, incidentally, are still going strong as founders, die-casters and engineers.

Below: Members of the Burnley Swimming Club pose proudly in this photograph of the Royal Life Saving Society's 'Award of Merit' Class in 1935. Swimming seems to have been a popular pastime of the 1930s and demand to use Burnley's public baths was great. Four had been built over the years, beginning with Albert Baths in 1863. Later, Central Baths was built in 1887. Gannow Baths (1902) and North Street Baths (1910) were twentieth century additions. Some swam for pleasure, or to keep fit, whilst others utilised their skills for the more serious purpose of saving lives.

To become a member of the Burnley Life Guard Corps required the passing of stringent tests as prescribed by the Royal Life Saving Society. A candidate had to win elementary and intermediate certificates, before going in for the bronze medallion. Success here brought entry into the elite Life Guard Corps.

It is possible that the six members of Burnley Swimming Club pictured here have just achieved this, for they have medallions on their costumes, although they might have won an even higher distinction.

Two years later, at their annual swimming gala, the Burnley Club demonstrated a new life-saving reel which had been provided by the RLSS. In case anyone wonders where members of the Lifeguard Corps practised their skills, they were supposed to report for duty at local beaches on their holidays. This was true devotion to duty!

It is 1914 at Turf Moor and the crowd is packed in behind the goal. This was the year that Burnley won the cup at the Crystal Palace, captained by Tommy Bogle. He was still the captain when, seven years later, Burnley won the old First Division championship and set up a record of 30 consecutive matches without defeat. Spectating was a rough and ready affair in 1914. There is not a crash barrier in sight and the fence looks positively flimsy. It was as well that lots of money was coming through the turnstiles, for judging by the solitary invitation to sample OXO, the club was not going to make a fortune from advertising revenue. The mammoth hoarding for putting up the half-time scores is empty, so this may well be a pre-match scene. One

can imagine the band entertaining the crowd, whilst four young boys progress around the ground, holding a sheet at each corner in which to collect the flying coppers. Things were different in so many ways, not least in the composition of the crowd. The game of 'spot the female' is quite a difficult one, although the smiling face of one lady is there, just to the right of the OXO sign. Obviously, for the most part, the men went to the match and the women saw to their domestic duties. In one way, this crowd scene of 1914 is a poignant one. It was the eve of the Great War and during the next few years a sizeable number of the men shown in this photograph would have gone to serve their country in France, never to return to the terraces of Turf Moor.

Happy anticipation shines in the faces of these youngsters as they eagerly await to depart on their outing. The scene is captured outside the Red Lion Street School in 1928. The purpose of the trip and the destination speak volumes for the times. The outing was organised by Pearson's Fresh Air Fund, Burnley Branch and the charabanc was heading for Whalley. Those prominent in the arranging of the excursion are pictured standing alongside the vehicle, with the leading light Alderman Buchanan on the far right. In 1928, fresh air was something of a scarce commodity in Northern mill towns, as factory and house chimneys continually pumped smoke into the sky. People who grew up in the North tended to assume that the blackness of their buildings was the natural colour of millstone grit, for even the moorland outcrops had been blackened by well over a century of industrial pollution. The 'miracle' of stone cleaning from the 70s, derided by some as artificial, revealed in fact the natural colour of the original stonework. Not that the problem was ignored in the 1920s, as the existence of Pearson's Fresh Air Fund proves. Some well-to-do people, who could more easily escape the town centres than the poorer classes, were concerned about the effects of the poisonous fumes. Charity committees warned of damaged lungs and stunted growth. Hence the trip to Whalley. It does not sound very far, or very exciting, but to most of these working-class children it was a distant, green oasis. It was an adventure to those who may have never ventured outside Burnley before. In any case, in a tightly packed charabanc, licensed to go at only 12mph, Whalley was probably far enough!

Above: What better way to enjoy the bracing air of Blackpool than by having a trip in an open charabanc? The photographer was at hand to record this little outing of Burnley people and the date was around 1929. The marvellous old charabanc belonged to Blackpool Corporation and so our Burnley holidaymakers were about to enjoy an open air tour around. When the ones who were standing had packed themselves in as well, they would need all the air they could get. The hard, wooden slatted seats and solid suspension would hardly have provided the height of comfort but no doubt these Burnley folk had a good time. They have certainly dressed for the occasion and the height of fashion is on display. It is curious how, right up to World War Two and beyond, almost everyone of whatever age wore some sort of headgear. It is almost startling when, as in this picture, someone appears bare-headed. This looks a reasonably well-to-do group of people, but holidaymaking came increasingly within more people's financial scope after the First World War. Blackpool and other West Coast resorts were the obvious popular choices. Probably we will never know the destination of this particular charabanc outing, but let's hope that it was not one of those Mystery Tours that ended up with them sitting in Towneley Park.

Right: We travel back to Edwardian times, 1910 to be precise, for this fine old photograph of the Well Hall Hotel. The view takes the eye along a section at Church Street which was to become Keirby Walk in the 1960s town centre redevelopment scheme. The hotel stood on the site of Well Hall, which had belonged to a Dr William Greenwood. Its lifetime as a public house spanned the years 1873 to 1958. Another public house can be spotted in the background, the White Lion in St James's Street, which was rebuilt in 1910. The Town Hall clock, standing at twenty minutes to six, looms in the background. The whole picture has an Edwardian feel about it, with the setts, the curving tram lines, the old-style property and the gas lamps. Life must have been a struggle for working-class families in Burnley at this time, but at least the Liberal Government of the day had introduced free school meals for needy children in 1906 and Lloyd George's old-age pensions were about to filter through to the poor, at the princely sum of 5 shillings [25p] per week. However, every little helped and 'God bless LORD George', was reputedly the cry of some of the first pensioners who, probably for the first time in their lives, were receiving 'something for nothing'.

Open spaces are vital to any town and this was particularly true of Burnley in the 1930s, when so much domestic and industrial smoke hung in the atmosphere. Very few people owned cars and so pleasures often had to be taken close to home at weekends and holiday time. On such occasions, local parks attracted people in their thousands in search of fresh air and a bit of fun. Therefore, it was money well employed when, in 1930, Burnley Corporation spent almost the entire amount of a £50,000 bequest from Mr James Witham Thompson on the creation of Thompson Park. It included a boating lake, a paddling pool, rose gardens, a conservatory, a tea room and almost unique for the time, an Italian garden. Shortly before the official opening, the park was thrown open to the public for the first time at Whitsuntide, 1930. The first photograph shows the massive public response, as crowds of children almost obliterate the paddling pool. It is difficult to spot a swimming costume, but plenty of enjoyment is being derived from simply dabbling the feet in water. A public holiday was a chance to dress up, rather than undress and some very fashionable cloche hats are on display. Away from the pool, hundreds of people are enjoying a leisurely stroll and the boating lake is attracting plenty of attention, especially from the spectators on the ornamental bridge in the distance.

During that first Whitsuntide weekend, from Saturday to Monday, it was claimed that the boating lake attracted 4,500 people. Rowing boats, skiffs, canoes and children's paddle boats packed the lake and attendants with megaphones had to constantly exhort the boaters to, 'keep left'. There were a few mishaps, generally from collisions with the stone embankment.

More than likely these were caused by young men displaying their rowing prowess to female spectators. Some things never change. However, the photograph of the lake shows a more tranquil occasion and as it is a postcard, the emphasis is on quiet pleasures and beautiful scenery.

At the official opening of Thompson Park, on July 16th 1930, civic dignitaries gathered in the tea room to thank Mr W Thompson, the brother of the late benefactor.

The Borough Engineer, Mr A Race, presented the Mayor, Alderman H R Nuttall J P, with a gold key with which to open the park gates. He commented on a problem which we associate with the modern day, rather than the 30s, when he spoke about 'ruffianism and wilful damage' having already taken place.

Later speakers played this down, blaming a few youths from outside Burnley who had simply come to 'show off'. Certainly the group of children queuing eagerly for the boats do not look like 'ruffians'. This was obviously one of the lake's busier days and these cheerful and lively youngsters could not wait to get at the boats. Eager they might have been, but they were not about to storm the lake, unless the girl at the front really meant business with that gate bolt. Working-class children of the 1930s were not fashion conscious, like the children of today are. They could not afford to be and so they dressed in whatever was available, but oh dear, those berets ...

Burnley Express

Above and left: These two photographs of the interior and exterior of the Travelling Library are dated 1936. The first free library in Burnley was the Marshall Library on Trafalgar Street, opened in 1914 and the Central Library was opened in 1930. Mobile libraries today are rarely seen outside rural areas, but Burnley Corporation was determined that the habit of reading and perhaps self-improvement, should reach all parts of the borough. Public transport was readily available to reach libraries, but the mobile library could help people to take that first vital step into the world of books, people whose experience of books at school may not have been a happy one. Also, the service must have been of great benefit to those with mobility difficulties, such as the sick and elderly. We are accustomed, of course, to a completely free book borrowing service, but 1d per volume, for 14 days, does not look a bad deal. In addition the cost of buying books in the 1930s was much greater in real terms because they were almost totally in hardback form. 'Penguin' paperbacks had only been launched in July 1935, at 6d per book and this was the first attempt to reach a mass market with good quality literature. Of the two gentlemen in the interior, one looks as if he has just come in to get out of the cold (nothing new there) whilst the other is deeply absorbed in 'The Gilded Halo' The shelves are skilfully arranged so that cornering did not result in the books themselves becoming too mobile and the articulated type vehicle would also have helped in this respect. What a useful vehicle also for manoeuvering a relatively large load around narrow streets.

Below: The Corporation Arms, in the area of the old Market Hall, had been a familiar sight since the nineteenth century.

Originally a house owned by one James Howarth, the business was in the hands of the Wilkinson family from around 1860 until its closure in 1967. By this latter date, the whole row of houses which was once attached to the Corporation Arms had gone and demolition lay in wait soon for the pub itself. The photograph was taken in 1963 and from the name of the pub it is easy to surmise that it began its life when Burnley was incorporated as a borough in 1861. Either that, or it changed its name and as if to punch the message home, a photograph of 1901 shows the arms of Burnley Corporation proudly painted on the whitewash. This very early photograph also shows that 'Massey's and Grimshaw's Sparkling Ales and Stouts' were the order of the day. By 1963, however, the Corporation declares itself to be 'Free from Brewer', although the word 'BASS' is clear enough on each side of the door. The Market Street nameplate is equally clear and although Market Hall traders and customers had plenty of choice in the vicinity, quite a few of them must have quenched their thirsts at the Corporation over the years. There used to be an old phrase about young people drinking 'corporation pop', ie water from the tap, if they complained of thirst. This might have had a completely different meaning in Burnley.

A fascinating story of social change lies in these two shots of the Palace Hippodrome, on St James's Street, taken only 10 years apart. The Palace, one of Burnley's famous town centre landmarks, had been built in 1907, amazingly in only five months. It was built as a theatre to seat over 2,000 people and its wonderful frontage bears all the hallmarks of the theatre architecture of the day.

Theatres have to adapt or die and like many others, the Palace coped with the competition from moving pictures by becoming a cinema itself. Nevertheless, the 1959 photograph shows some of the theatre tradition still alive in the shape of the large poster advertising the visit of the Prachewsky Ensemble, dancers of Czechoslovakia and the Palace was home to the Burnley Light Opera Society between 1958 and 1964. Below the poster, we can see the two films advertised very plainly. Sal Mineo was a well-known star of the day, although the film 'Tonka' was not one that people talked about for years to come. Again, neither 'Darby O'Gill and the Little People', nor its star Albert Sharpe, have passed into folk memory. Interestingly, however, buried away among the minor credits is the name of Sean Connery, before he became better known as 007, James Bond. So much for what was happening at the Palace in 1959, but the 'FOR SALE' sign on the premises to the right has some significance for the

changes about to come.

So much has been said and written about the physical change in the centre of Burnley that it is easy to overlook the social changes that often underlie them. The date is now 1969 and the Palace has had to adapt again. BINGO was one of the crazes that was sweeping across the nation in the 60s and in common with many cinemas, the Palace had become a Bingo Hall. Cinemas found it difficult to face the challenge of television and picture houses in the 1950s rarely had the facilities to attract people out of their warm living rooms. But Bingo offered something different - a chance to win a fortune!

Bingo Halls became spectacularly successful at drawing people out of their homes and not just because it was a little 'flutter'. The sign on the Palace described itself in 1969 as a Social Club, which meant that groups of housewives in particular could view the whole experience as a social occasion. Films might be watched in silence, often in solitude. Not so the cheerful, chatty outing to Bingo. The 1959 photograph showed a 'FOR SALE' sign and by 1969 these premises were occupied by Tesco, indicating another social trend, ie the huge change in our shopping habits and the growth of supermarkets. The Palace, after passing through its many phases, was demolished in 1973 as part of the Palace Block Development.

Christmas at the Junior Library, Burnley, is the theme for these fascinating shots of 1947 and 1957. Libraries use a variety of imaginative devices to introduce children to the world of books, but what a splendid idea to have a Christmas Tree decorated with books. This was in 1947 and librarian Richard Caul is encouraging the children to examine the titles on display. These make for some interesting reading. The girl on the left is holding 'Lord of the Jungle,' whilst the one on the right, with the scarf around her head, seems to favour the 'Christmas Book'. The librarian himself is pointing out 'Jim Davis' and further up the tree hangs the 'Junior Film Annual'. Nineteen forty seven was still very much a time of post-war austerity, with rationing still in force and restrictions on any number of things, including the supply of paper. Books were not really in plentiful supply. The children of working-class parents could hang up their pillowcases on Christmas Eve and find the next morning that their entire batch of presents comfortably fitted inside. It was not uncommon to find an orange or a banana at the bottom, fruits which had become luxuries during the war. With luck, there might also be a book, something to be treasured and read over and over again.

Ten years on and life had changed for the better in material terms. 'You've never had it so good', stated Harold MacMillan at about this time and in many ways he was right. The quantity and variety of goods in shops was enormous compared with 1947 and ordinary people's real incomes had risen too. This is reflected in the photograph of 1957. Once again it is Christmas at the Junior Library, but there seems to be a greater degree of prosperity evident. Children were beginning to think in terms of two or three pillowcases by Christmas Eve 1957. What a cheerful bunch of smiling faces greet the cameraman, but that may be due, of course, to the proximity of Father Christmas. It is likely that his sack is somewhere near by, full of books. In this respect, he could well have handed out the titles of 1947, for children's tastes in books had not changed a great deal. The days of Raymond Briggs and Roald Dahl were yet to come.

Burnley Express

Even in the 1990s, with all the stay-at-home attractions of videos and computers, funfairs still have a compelling attraction for youngsters. For those who are young no more, it is easy to remember how the pulse quickened at the sound of the music and the sight of the bright lights against the night sky. Excitement hung in the air and the pace of your steps inevitably quickened. Although night time is really the only time to savour the atmosphere of the fair, this photograph of the Burnley Fair at Hill Top in 1951 conveys something of the swirl of activity. The famous fairground name of Shaw can be seen a little way to the left of the thrilling looking helter-skelter. At bottom right, the picture below the Mitchell sign makes it very
likely that the dodgems await up the steps. The old Cattle Market used to be the site of the fair, but this was earmarked for development by the early 50s. The Hill Top site, featured, is occupied now by Sion Baptist Church and Sainsbury's. The fair has moved on to Fulledge Recreation Ground. Venues may change, but memories of fairs are always much the same, made up of a medley of sound, movement and colour. Who will ever forget the heave of the speedway, the arrogant strut of the fairground youths across the boards, or the piercing screams of girls as the waltzers were spun ever more rapidly? For others, the memories might be of the sparks cracking at the tops of the dodgem poles, or that first sweet mouthful of candy floss.

This view of the Savoy Cafe and Cinema, complete with famous dome, must rank high in the nostalgia ratings for Burnley folk of a certain generation. What a landmark it was along Manchester Road, as seen in June 1953. The Savoy was opened in 1922, to seat 1,100 people, in the days of the silent film. The cinema was the first in Burnley to show 'talkies', in 1929. After that, the resident piano accompanist must have become increasingly redundant. The dominance of the film was so great in a pre-television world that the Palace Theatre of Varieties and the Empire Music Hall had to convert to the new crowd pulling medium. Right into the 1950s cinemas were drawing good audiences and it was not uncommon to have to queue round the block. There were enough customers to make it financially worthwhile to show a film twice in an evening, as well as having a daily matinee as the 'TIMES' board, outside the Savoy, indicates. Nevertheless, the Savoy had closed by 1956 and the building was demolished in 1958. A branch of Martins Bank was then built on the site and this in turn has been replaced to make way for more change. The activity on the photograph suggests midday, or thereabouts, for a good many more people are clustered around the confectionery and cafe part of the Savoy than around the cinema entrance. The little pedal scooter parked outside the cinema was quite a common sight in the 50s. They always seemed to involve more 'pedal' than 'scoot'.

Burnley Express

Below: The Empress Ballroom is seen here just about on the verge of completion. It opened on December 1st 1927, on the site of the Pavilion Picture Hall and its fine frontage became a familiar sight over the years to thousands of Burnley folk who were out for a good night. The Empress represented the height of modernity in 1927 and its publicity spoke of the 'up-to-date and magnificently appointed ballroom', with room for 600 dancers. Nor were the rowdier elements going to be allowed to spoil the fun. The phrase, 'strict supervision in the Hall', no doubt meant the 1920s equivalent of 'bouncers'. For forty years the Empress was the focal point in Burnley for large-scale social functions, roller-skating and above all, dancing. The culture of the dance hall as the place where the opposite sex could get together has all but vanished with the advent of the disco. The major problem for the young men of the time was that success depended on their ability both to dance and to engage in witty conversion. Neither of these applies to the disco; an ability to lip-read will do. The Empress was the place where the young men of Burnley were put to the test in the mysteries of the foxtrot and conversational skills which went beyond 'Do you come here often?' Many passed the test and the Empress was the place that set many a romance in motion. Countless happy hours were spent there and it was a sad loss when the Empress was destroyed by fire in 1962.

Bottom: This shot of the Royal Oak Hotel, on St James's Street, was taken around 1929. It was originally a house, like so many of the old public houses and basked in the glory of being described by Edwin Lutyens, the famous architect, as Burnley's best designed building. Doubtless the locals were less interested in its aesthetic appearance than in the quality of 'Grimshaw's sparkling ales', not to mention their 'noted stouts' and 'genuine wines and spirits'. Has any pubic house ever sold any beverage that was not 'noted', or the 'finest' or 'award winning'? The policeman seems to have hung his cape on the wall and donned a white coat. Perhaps he was about to go on traffic duty, a reminder of just how far back our traffic problems go. On leaving the 'Royal Oak', if any spare money happened to be jingling in the pocket, one could spend it at the

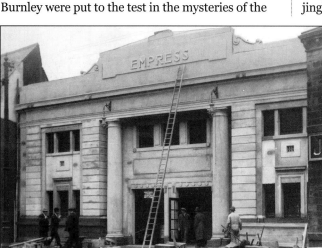

Dining Rooms visible in the picture, or pick up a 'Bargain' or 'Reduction' at the shop which is clearly closing down. The 1920s were hard times in Lancashire, with foreign competition playing havoc with the textiles industry and harder times lay ahead, with the Wall Street Crash of 1929, in the USA, precipitating the industrial world into depression and the 'hungry thirties'. There would have been little money to spare in the Burnley of 1929. This could have been the reason for the 'Closing Down', or perhaps the proprietor had spent too long sampling next door's 'sparkling ales'. The 'Royal Oak' itself closed down in 1931, to make way for the building of Marks and Spencer on its site.

Storytime at Lanehead School in 1969 and the children listen spellbound to Miss Marshall - well almost. One or two are stealing suspicious or curious looks at the camera. Almost 30 years on and many of these tots will have their own tots in school now. In 1969, Mr Ken Happer was head of the school, which was closely linked to St John's Church at Briercliffe. Lanehead grew out of a Sunday School, becoming a day school in 1834. Old schools always have a fund of good stories and apparently at one time the head used to live in the school and had a bed in the corner of a classroom, a fate fortunately not shared by Mr Happer. Also, long ago, a large and ancient cupboard existed in one classroom, known as the 'Bogy Hole'

and it may have been used to literally shut up noisy children. A browse through the school log book would not give anyone much of a desire to return to the 'turn of the century' when ringworm, diphtheria and scarlet fever were fairly common ailments among children. Now, of course, we can look back to 1969 and only marvel at the changes lived through by the children on this photograph. Everyone would have their own personal choice, as to the most important one, but the rise of the microchip and the computer must surely be a strong contender in terms of shaping the world in which these children would live. However some things remain much the same and a story from 'miss' or 'sir' is still a good way to end the school day.

Burnley Express

Above: The walls of junior school classrooms seemed to get brighter and more cheerful in the 1960s and the children's art work forms a pleasant backdrop to this photograph taken at St Andrew's School, in September 1969. At this time, Mr H Holdsworth was the head and the school had celebrated its centenary in 1967. Eight of the 160 pupils are seen here seated around the communal table, looking as neat and tidy as the table settings themselves. Dinnertime was imminent and no doubt these young ladies were about to enjoy their eating and socialising under the benevolent eye of their teacher. Free school meals for needy children began as a national policy in 1906, but by 1944 they had become subsidised meals, open to all at the same price. With such a long history, memories of school dinners are bound to be mixed. For some, they might be remembered as the best meal of the day and some schools even provided dinners in the holidays for the children of working parents. For others, the abiding memory is of sponge pudding and lumpy custard; food barons at the top of the table and starving peasants at the bottom. By 1969 the cafeteria system had been established, a great improvement by which children took their trays to the counter and enjoyed a choice for each course. Therefore it is a fair bet that these children of St Andrew's would in future years look back with fond memories of the food served up to them by Mrs Cotter, Mrs Johnson and Mrs Redfearn.

Top: The first Free Library in Burnley was the Marshall Library on Trafalgar Street, opened in 1914. The present Central Library opened in 1930 and the scene is a busy day in the Junior Department. The photograph must have been taken before 1937, for at that point this spacious room started to be used as a lecture hall. The thirst for knowledge is very apparent and it is pretty much standing room only. From the uniforms on view, it is clear that a school party has arrived and congestion is heavy at the doorway. How was the strict rule of 'SILENCE' enforced? School trips to public libraries were very popular at this time. The idea was to foster the reading habit and to encourage children who might not have any access to books at home, to begin to use the library. Such trips still take place and of course you might well be visiting a library today with a view to borrowing a video as much as a book. The photograph has some interesting features as to decor, especially the high backed chairs and in the foreground, those charming old-fashioned sloping reading desks. These had a very handy ledge underneath, both for storing books and for banging the knees. Also the coat rack in the middle of the room has been very obediently used. One intriguing question remains and it concerns the girl in the foreground with her cheek resting against her hand. Is she deep in thought, or has she quietly gone to sleep?

Above: The Vic, on St James's Street, photographed in 1953, closed in 1955 and so to some it may simply mean a name from the past. To others, however, the name is extremely evocative, bringing recollection of a truly great era in the history of the live theatre of Burnley. The Victoria Assembly Room was built in 1886 and was soon to become the Victoria Theatre or, more fondly, the Vic. It embraced drama, opera, ballet and pantomime and the renowned Madame Adelina Patti sang at the very first performance. In the early days, Mr W C Horner was instrumental in bringing world famous names to appear at the Vic. The Italian Opera Company performed there, as did D'Oyly Carte. Undoubtedly, however, the great years of the Vic belonged to the Second World War. The silver lining in an otherwise grim situation was, that to escape the London Blitz, the Old Vic made the Burnley Vic its headquarters, bringing with it the Sadler's Wells Opera and Ballet Companies. In January 1941, an eight week season of opera, ballet and drama was launched and a stunning array of talent appeared before Burnley audiences. One wonders what is the most enduring memory for those who had the privilege to be there? Is it Shakespeare, as performed by Sybil Thorndike and Tyrone Guthrie; is it the grace of Margot Fonteyn; or is it the majestic music of Mozart and Verdi? Surely nobody in 1941 could have guessed that professional theatre had only 14 years left to run in Burnley.

Below: The Thorn Hotel on St James's Street, with its whitewashed walls, must have been a delightful spot for popping in to have a quick one. Of course you could stay longer in this popular residential establishment, whose courtyard gave a pleasant and secluded feel to the place. To complete an attractive picture, the trees in leaf offered a little summer shade. The smart looking car indicates the 1960s, but it would have to be the earlier part, for all this was swept away in the re-development of that decade. Along with the hotel went Hargreaves's The Tobacconist, and Zip. The latter was a dry cleaning firm which would clean a coat for 4s 6d (22½p) and so we really are somewhere in the 60s. Massey was a Burnley concern, with its brewery at Westgate and it had a reputation which went well outside the boundaries of the town. Another local name was Grimshaw's, with a brewery at Cliviger, although it was not quite so well known outside Burnley. As these breweries closed, it seemed inevitable that a few national giants would dominate the industry, offering little variety or choice. All was not lost for the dedicated beer drinker. The Campaign for Real Ale, or CAMRA, demanded the return of hand-pulled ales, with a variety of taste. This display of consumer power persuaded entrepreneurs to set up small, independent breweries, concentrating on a local area. Hence we now have not Massey's, but Moorhouse's of Burnley, with its Premier and Pendle Witch brews.

AUTHOR AND SUBJECT CATALOGUE.

Links between local schools and public lending libraries have always been seen as very important. Libraries are a vast resource for opening up children's minds to other worlds, not just the world of facts and knowledge, but also that of the imagination. At its most basic level, libraries can help children with their schoolwork. The Burnley Central Library has always been conscious of its role in this respect and has forged links with local schools in many ways. In the first place children have to know how to find the book they want and this photograph of 1952 shows Christine Ralph, the Children's Librarian, demonstrating how to use the catalogue. The girls are all giving due attention and probably the one on the right will soon be having a go herself. The next step then, of course, will be to use the reference number to locate the book on the shelves. So, no more wandering around aimlessly when they next visit the library to get some help with their homework. The girls are very much in the school uniforms of the day. There are one or two belted gaberdine raincoats on view, plus the old-fashioned satchels. When did anyone last see one of those? Then, of course, there is the ubiquitous beret, surely the most unflattering piece of female headgear ever devised, no matter at what angle worn. Nevertheless, for these girls to be caught near school without their berets on, would probably merit a detention.

It's glasses raised to the 'Clarets' as the Mayor, Councillor Miss Edith Utley, clinks glasses with the Burnley FC Captain, Jimmy Adamson, to celebrate the winning of the First Division title in 1960. This was the first championship for Burnley for 39 years, the title having been clinched in a nail-biting final game at Maine Road against Manchester City. Burnley had a magnificent team in the early 60s, renowned for brilliant free-flowing football which earned them admirers throughout the land. It is worth asking why a small mill town could produce such a team. Burnley never had the resources to buy big name, 'ready made' footballers, but in this apparent problem lay the key to success. The club developed a wide ranging network of talent scouts who brought good young footballers to Turf Moor. This youth policy, perhaps most evident in the North East, was highly successful and would later be copied by other clubs. Burnley also wisely invested in superb training facilities at Gawthorpe. In the 1960-61 season, Burnley reached the quarter-finals of the European Cup and the semi-final of the FA Cup. The following season, Burnley reached the final of the FA Cup and practically threw away the League title when they seemed to have it within their grasp. Some of the stars of that great team are pictured. John Connelly and Brian Miller raise their glasses on the left, with Roy Pointer's smiling face visible between them. On the far right stands Tommy Cummings. It was a privilege to watch these vintage 'Clarets', a once in a lifetime team.

Burnley Express

Above: In 1962 it was reported that a £250,000 luxury Ten-Pin Bowling Centre was to be opened at Finsley Gate, Burnley, with 24 lanes. In 1963, this centre duly opened and the players pictured are all no doubt hoping for a 'strike'. As with everything else, ten-pin bowling looked easier than it actually was. Apart from the weight of the bowls, there was that peculiar backward-facing finger grip and the difficulty of curving the bowl down the lane in that graceful arc that was needed for a 'strike'. At least you did not have to go and fetch the bowls again. A machine obligingly regurgitated them on to the ramp at the side. In essence, the game was not all that new. There were Skittle Alleys in Victorian public houses. However, in the 60s, this new version of skittles came in from the USA with a fanfare of publicity and Bowling Centres opened up all over Britain. It was to be the new bright game of the 'Swinging Sixties' and at first it went through a boom time. It was tremendously popular and leagues sprang up everywhere. However, its fortunes have fluctuated since that early 'honeymoon' period. Perhaps the English only like bowling games that last four days and where the bowler can bowl with a 'short leg'

and a 'long leg' at the same time. The Ten-Pin Bowling Centre at Finsley Gate has had its own varying fortunes, but the game is going strong at present and offers one of the few opportunities locally to get that elusive 'strike'.

Top: Anyone who watched football in the near darkness of a late November afternoon in the early 1950s, will appreciate what the introduction of floodlighting did for the game. Turf Moor is shown here under floodlights in 1960 during a game against local rivals Blackburn Rovers. Some clubs were reluctant to face the cost, but the prospect of night football opened up exciting possibilities in terms of attendances. For example, cup replays need not be played on midweek afternoons, when many people could not attend because of work commitments. Grounds have changed out of all recognition since 1960, not always for the best reasons. Hooliganism in the 1970s led to the introduction of railings and pens to segregate home and away supporters. This prevented that huge trek of humanity that used to take place at half-time, when supporters moved in order to be at the 'attacking' end. New stands were built and Burnley FC tried hard to create a ground in keeping with the great name of the club. The Bob Lord Stand, named after the Burnley Chairman, was opened in 1974. From around 1970, Burnley's fortunes on the field went into decline and they have struggled for far too long in the lower divisions. However, the ambition of the club and its supporters is reflected in the modern Turf Moor all-seater stadium, which contains excellent facilities. Nevertheless, many regret the passing of the Open End, as featured in one picture and the terrific atmosphere that used to be engendered by those who stood on the 'Longside'.

Around the town centre

Above: A solitary workman on top of a half demolished building seems to be the only sign of human life in this picture of Church Street in 1938, but there is plenty elsewhere to remind us of what life was like just prior to the Second World War. Setts and tramlines, for instance, were common enough, even though the trams had stopped running in 1935. That was a nice tramline intersection at the junction, although a tricky one for cyclists. Advertisers, then as now, were not slow to see an opportunity. Although it might by easy to miss the faded 'Rowntrees Pastilles' sign above the Dining Rooms on the left, the demolition site hoardings have been plastered with eye-catching invitations to spend money in a variety of ways. These give a fascinating insight into the time. Theatre and cinema were flourishing, judging by the tempting offerings at the Pentridge, the Empire, the Vic and the Tivoli. Perhaps you could stroll along to the Empire, to see Bobby Breen in 'Rainbow on the River' and the following evening visit the Vic, to enjoy 'Sunshine Sally'. The rest of the advertisements concentrate on drinking, eating and smoking. There are some familiar names there and it is hard to believe that 'My Goodness, My Guinness' goes back as far as 1938. The name Gibbs may strike a chord for those who remember pre-tube toothpaste. Gibbs came in little round tins - blue, green or red - which contained a pink block of toothpaste. For many, these served as their first introduction to teeth cleaning.

Above right: A split-screen Morris Minor nosing its way into the picture and the dress of the pedestrians strongly suggests the 1950s in this photograph of Manchester Road. The Morris Minor and the later Austin Mini were in the vanguard of the car 'revolution' which brought the pleasures (and pains) of motoring to ordinary working people. The growth

of private transport was one of the key developments of the post-war years and was largely responsible for the reshaping of our towns and cities. The creation of small, reasonably priced family cars and the availability of credit facilities, saw a huge growth in car ownership. The nose of this humble Morris is pointing towards the ring-roads and motorways of the future. Humble or not, it would fetch a nice price in the vintage car market now. All the more so if it happened to be the Morris Traveller, that rather exotic wooden framed vehicle that was once famously described as a 'half-timbered car'. On the left of the picture, a cluster of shoppers has congregated near the Savings Bank and the New Day bedding and furniture shop. The Burton's building at the junction with St James's Street is the main landmark, with famous white frontage. The old Bull Inn once stood on this spot and had the distinction of being the foremost hotel in Burnley, hosting many important social functions. Burton's would have looked the epitome of modernity when it was opened in 1939. Sixty years on and it increasingly represents a symbol of stability amongst all the changes that have gone on around it.

This view of Manchester Road, taken in 1950, has all the hallmarks of the day in terms of the buildings and vehicles in view. The corner of Manchester Road and Grimshaw Street is dominated by the Barclays Bank building. It was built in 1894 and generations of industrial dirt and grime tended to hide the fact that it was a fine and solid edifice, built in the best Victorian traditions. The stonework of all Northern towns and cities suffered in much the same way and the corrosive effects of acid rain were part of the deadly pollution 'cocktail'. People more-or-less accepted that black was the normal colour of stonework. The beneficial effects of Clean Air Acts, along with the wonders of sand-blasting, have transformed many old building to their original colour and in the process their architec-tural features have been highlighted. A case in point is this Barclays Bank branch of 1950. A much cleaner version stands there now, although no longer used by Barclays. Further down the street, it is easy to spot the familiar dome of the Savoy Cinema which, sadly, was demolished in 1958. In the distance, the frontages of Dunkerley's and Addison's are visible which were well-known to shoppers of the 1950s. Dunkerley's sold shoes and Addison's sold wine and spirits. Both disappeared in the pedestrianisation of this central area in the 1960s. The vehicles on view in the photograph very much belong to the time and the heavy wagon rumbling up Manchester Road seems to be laden with sacks of coal, which brings us full circle back to blackened buildings.

Burnley Express

This photograph was rather symbolic when it was published in 1958. Mature readers will soon recognise the location as the roof of the Keirby Hotel, a modern concrete and steel structure built at the very dawn of the work to build the modern Burnley we know today. The picture will not be enjoyed by people prone to vertigo, and we can only admire the resolve of the workmen carrying out the construction work at this dizzy height. Interestingly, the men are not wearing hard hats. It is unlikely that they would be allowed to work unprotected on a modern construction site. The Keirby Hotel was built on a site formerly occupied by the Kierby Brewery, from which it took its name.

the centre of the picture have noticed the photographer at work and are staring at the camera. There jobs would change only three years after the picture was taken as a consequence of the phasing out of trams in 1935. Their fate had been sealed when more efficient and versatile motorbuses arrived on the scene in 1924.

Left: Men can be seen working on the 'Keep Left' sign in the middle of the photograph as a Rover saloon whooshes by on the left. This was Burnley's St. James's Street as it appeared before the major retail developments of the 1960s would transform the appearance of the area completely. Burton's the successful tailoring business operated from Leeds can be seen on the left. The imposing white facade of the property followed the style adopted by the firm in scores of towns and cities throughout Britain. It was opened by Britain's most successful tailors in 1939. Their success is legend and countless local men will have fond memories of their first Burtons suit and the weddings, interviews and 'first jobs' associated with it.

Top: This 1930s scene shows the centre of Burnley and several elements of the pubic transport system which served the town before most families had access to a private car. The scene was actually captured in 1932 and shows the Burton building with its clean white walls in the distance. The Transport Offices were located on the right of the picture with their distinctive clock showing 11.00 a.m. Several passengers and transport staff on the traffic island virtually in

Left: This photograph of St James's Street is bound to awaken memories for Burnley folk who liked to get about town in the early 1950s. The Palace clock was a common rendezvous place and then there was choice of entertainment, or if you felt 'flush' you could take them all in. Firstly, perhaps some refreshment at the BSK Cafe. The windows clearly show 'Luncheons' on the first floor and a 'Smoke Room' on the top floor. After that you could go to the pictures at the Palace and featuring on the particular day that this shot was taken was Danny Kaye in 'Hans Christian Anderson'. In case of emergency, the public toilets were very handy. It you were lucky enough to own one of the 'vintage' Fords shown in the picture, you could more-or-less leave it where you liked. Yellow lines were unheard of at this date. The cars, of course, were technically crude by modern standards, but they did possess one small advantage. If the engine was troublesome in starting, you could always get out the old starting handle and give it a good crank up. This view of the Cafe and Palace has now vanished into the mind's eye and the store of happy memories. The Palace Block development completed in 1979, now offers a completely different view, with not a car in sight.

Above: The magnificent sight of thousands of cheering, well-behaved Burnley football supporters greeted the team bus as it toured the town in April 1947. The occasion related to the Wembley Cup Final of that year when Burnley were defeated by Charlton Athletic by one goal to nil in extra time. the picture was taken from the steps of the Town Hall looking up Manchester Road. The tall building in the background is the old fire station. A band can be seen playing in the foreground of the picture - and a mounted police officer in the distance carefully nudges members of the crowd back into position in support of his colleagues. This would be done more out of concern for their safety than any worries about public order. the picture made a good advert for *Eastwoods Luxury Coaches* and it is possible to make out individual members of the cup final team protruding through the open sun roof. Alan Brown, the captain, Harry Potts, Harold Mather, George Bray, Jimmy Strong and Reg Attwell are all there, with the Mayor wearing his chain of office in the centre.

Above: High flat roofs, low flat roofs, steep gable ends with mini-spires and the strange projecting feature at Dodsley's - all part of the medley of styles that characterised this part of Yorkshire Street in the 1950s. Such a wealth of structural styles in a small area is unusual even for that pre-development year, but there was always some variety to be found. This was because people were building for different purposes at different times, thus escaping the uniformity of a large-scale building project. Even the electric lighting has an unusual appearance. The photograph was taken on the corner of Morton Street, looking towards the centre and prominent on the right is the Sion Baptist Church, with its solid appearance. Facing up the street is the Black and White Cafe and next to it the fascinating frontage of Dodsley's. This dispensing and photographic shop proudly lets all-comers know that it sells, amongst other things, 'D Brand Quick Acting Aspirin Tablets' and 'Uric Solvets for Rheumatism'. Their 'Albo Cream' seemingly cured chapped hands. You positively yearn to enter the door and rummage around, confident that whatever your ailment the cure will be there. The demolition and rebuilding work of the late 1950s and early 1960s, which produced Keirby Walk, transformed this varied scene. Sion Baptist Church was rebuilt at Hill Top in Church Street.

Above right: This view of Yorkshire Street is no more, for it pre-dates the Keirby Block development of the late 50s and early 60s which changed the area out of all recognition. However, the style of dress and type of vehicles indicate that the pre-dating is not by much. There is a bustle of activity and traffic seems light considering the number of pedestrians. Clearly this was a popular little shopping area, offering a fair range of goods and services. Leeder's Electrical Services feature prominently on the right and there is something curiously modern in the sales promotion displayed in the window. The claim that '100 Hoovers Must Be Won' would not seem out of place in a modern locally based sales campaign. Further up the street, to the left, the white building houses the spacious upstairs rooms of Boardman's Furnishers. Coming down the street from this point, there is the almost irresistible temptation to sample Barker's and Dobson's chocolates and sweets. Below this, the shop with the rather nice columns was the home of Britannic Assurance. Whatever else might be said of the shopping streets of yesteryear, visually they did offer a variety of styles and sizes. This was partly because the buildings were often erected at different times and partly because some of them were built as houses. Shopping malls and superstores offer a tremendous range of goods over a relatively compact area, but their uniformity of style offers little of interest on the outside.

The Co-operative Building on Hammerton Street, here pictured in 1970, is an example of the good quality of Victorian architecture, as applied to public buildings and to the private residences of the better off. This did not apply, of course, to the rows of terraces which were 'thrown up' for the working classes and which soon became slums. The founding of the Co-operative Movement, however, was aimed at helping just such people. The Rochdale Pioneers of 1844 aimed at buying and selling cheaply for their members, with any profits distributed as dividends. The idea spread quickly and by 1860 Burnley had its first Co-operative shop. It prospered in Burnley, if the evidence of this fine building is anything to go by and in spite of fierce competition in retailing, the Co-operative Movement marches on. Thomas Hughes, the author of 'Tom Brown's Schooldays', laid the memorial stone for the Hammerton Street building in 1885 and it is well worth examining its stonework, arched windows and balustrades. On the photograph, the Co-operative Bank is on the right, with the old British Rail logo prominent further down the street. There is a tablet and inscription high on the building, to the right. It is a puzzle as to why an inscription should be placed in a position where only the starlings, sparrows and pigeons can read it.

It would be easy to say that this aerial view of Burnley, taken in August 1960, was one of a town on the eve of change and it is true that the photograph precedes the substantial redevelopment of the centre which took place in the 1960s and 1970s. However, towns are under a constant process of change. For example, this view would have been difficult to capture at all in an earlier decade, when uncontrolled emissions from factory chimneys threw a smoke haze over the town. Also, one substantial construction was already in place by 1960, the building containing the new law courts and police station. This was built on the site of the old Cattle market and bus station and was opened in 1955. It can be seen to the bottom right of the picture. Again, the Savoy Cinema was demolished in 1958 and so its famous dome does not grace this photograph. However, radical changes to the town centre began in ernest in the 1960s. Taking the white building of Burton's as a reference point, almost in the centre of the photograph, those who know Burnley well will be able to examine the area around St James's Street. This is where the re-development was so intense and it is possible to do a 'then and now' comparison from the picture. Many felt that the heart had been torn out of Burnley. This is understandable, but the heart of a town does not lie in buildings. It lies in the close bonds that are forged between people who live, work and play together. In this sense, the heart of Burnley beats as strongly as ever.

Below: It's quiet day on Howe Street in 1963, as two policemen pass the time of day. By this date, it was unusual to see a Burnley Street scene in which the policemen almost outnumbered the cars. Maybe more were about to pour down the street, or perhaps it was just a quiet time of day. There are some traditional high gable ends on the skyline and some 'anti-sleepwalking' iron guard rails on several of the upper windows. The names along the street may jog the memories of those who used to shop along here in the early 60s.

One name with wider associations than Howe Street and even than with Burnley itself, is that of Lord's Butchers. Bob Lord started his working life selling meat from a barrow on the streets of Burnley. He later built up a chain of butchers' shops, but his real passion was for Burnley Football Club. Mr Lord became chairman of the club in 1955 and remained at the helm until shortly before his death in 1981.

On the wider football stage, he had prominent positions in both the Football League and the Football Association. Bob Lord was an outspoken man, with forthright opinions. He had his admirers and detractors, in equal numbers, but his importance to the local club is commemorated by the Bob Lord Stand at Turf Moor.

This view of Howe Street could as well belong to the 50s as the 60s, but for one detail. The invitation to step inside the 'Continental Ladies and Gentlemen's Hair Stylists' is surely a 'sign' of the times. Such sophistication belonged to the 'Swinging Sixties'.

Right: The Old Red Lion Hotel, at the very heart of Burnley, in Manchester Road, gives a glimpse of the past in the solid appearance of its architecture. It still stands proudly on its corner, seemingly untouched by the changes that have gone on about it.

A great deal of the twentieth century history of Burnley has ebbed and flowed outside its doors and the event being celebrated here was the Coronation of 1953. In common with many public and private buildings in Burnley, a good effort has been made to decorate in suitably patriotic style, with bunting, flags and the 'ER' emblem. Alas, as so often happens on important occasions, the weather did its best to be totally out of keeping with the event . June 2nd 1953 was dull and cold and by the evidence of this photograph, a little wet too. The headscarves and raincoats give the appearance of a gusty Autumn day, not the height of Summer. Nevertheless, the Old Red Lion is still a fine sight, with the impressive doorway to the right and some ornate carvings above the seemingly redundant doorway in the middle. The left-hand section is a little different and looks as if it may have either undergone alterations, or been 'tacked on' at a later date. However the tiling inside the doorway is very much in keeping with a traditional public house.

Somewhere high up in St Peter's Church gave a superb vantage point for this shot of the Talbot Hotel and Sparrow Hawk Inn in 1951. History in abundance lay below, for this was the very oldest part of the town, where the original market was held. The Sparrow Hawk was the crest of the Towneleys and it is known that an inn has stood on the site of the Sparrow Hawk since the Middle Ages. Neither of the buildings on the photograph go back as far as that, but they have that solid and substantial look which now appears to belong to a completely different age. Style is a personal thing, but surely these old buildings were built 'in style'. In a sense, time too is a personal thing. For younger

people, 1951 is practically half a century ago and could well seem almost as far away as the Middle Ages. For older people 1951 was only yesterday, just around the corner in time. Where did all the years go? One clue to the age of the picture is the style of the cars which are visible. Another is the convoy of prams trundling across the setts.

The large-scale and sturdy prams are positively vintage now and seem like battleships alongside modern small-wheeled buggies. Nineteen fifty-one was a turning point year in one respect. It was the year of the Festival of Britain and the attempt to wrench Britain out of its post-war hangover and point it to the future.

Left: The old inter-town bus station, on Parker Lane had once been the cattle market and this photograph of around 1950 captures the whole area in pre-development days. The buses are the old-fashioned open backed type and one remembers the conductor as being 'king' of the platform, with his money bag slung over one shoulder and his ticket machine over the other. If you missed one of these buses, there was a chance of catching it at the first junction and leaping on board. The reverse process, the casual dropping off at a corner, was strictly for the 'show off' types and sometimes ended in humiliation. Opposite the bus station, one can see a period piece motor car parked along the row which contains Waterproofs and the 'Rose and Thistle Hotel'. One of the most eye-catching features of the background is the distinctive white facade of Burton's, opened in 1939 on the site of the old 'Bull Inn', which used to describe itself as the principal hotel in Burnley. Burton's had many buildings like this throughout the country and in terms of getting noticed, it was a successful marketing exercise. Another instantly recognisable feature in 1950 was the dome of the Savoy Theatre, which can clearly be seen. The Savoy, opened only in 1922, would close in 1956 and be demolished in 1958. If the Burnley skyline was soon to change, there were more immediate plans for the bus station. On this site, the foundation stone for the new law courts and police station was laid in 1952 and the new building opened in 1955.

Below: This view of Market Street looking towards Standish Street has an early 'sixtyish' look about it, judging from the array of vehicles in view. The ever popular Mini and Morris Minor immediately catch the eye. Clearly the age of the car had dawned, with all its associated problems of parking and street congestion. Probably less was known by the public of the poisonous effects of traffic fumes, for this was rarely mentioned as a problem in those days. The Burnley town centre re-development was, in part, a response to the congestion typified by this photograph. The result was to be the pedestrian precincts, inner ring-roads and large car parks which, so radical at the time, are now such a common feature of our towns and cities. Familiar signs on the right-hand side of Market Street are those of Altham's Stores and 'Massey's Ales and Stouts'. The latter, attached to the rather plain exterior of the New Market Hotel, is a reminder of the once famous brewery, which has disappeared from the landscape. It was once thought inevitable that beer production would eventually be concentrated in a few powerful hands, but thanks to the consumers' demands for 'real ale', a host of small, independent brewers have sprung up in order to suit every refinement of the beer connoisseur's taste.

Below: The imposing grandeur of the Town Hall is the first thing to catch the eye in this photograph taken from Centenary Way. The Town Hall was opened in 1888, during the reign of Queen Victoria and it bears all the hallmarks of the municipal buildings of that age. It would not be true to say that local councils had 'money to burn' in those days, but they seemed to have enough public money to erect truly magnificent buildings. They used good quality materials and employed the best architects and craftsmen. Probably there was some element of competition between councils and this municipal pride was often supplemented by private subscriptions from wealthy individuals, provided that they got a mention somewhere. Opposite the Town Hall is the shape of things to come as Chaddersley House, the new home of the Social Services Department, is coming into being. This was a 1960s development and as Brunswick Methodist Chapel was demolished in 1963 as part of it, this gives us a clue to the date. More 60s evidence can be gleaned from the cluster of cars close to the petrol station and in front of Hirst, Ibbetson and Taylor Ltd. One is certainly a 'Baby' Austin and at a guess, there is an Austin Cambridge to the left and a white Ford Consul in front of the sign. The experts will soon sort this one out and identify the other two cars for good measure.

Right: Old rubs shoulders with the new seems to sum up this aerial view of the Keirby Roundabout in 1962, just after its completion. The 1960s redevelopment scheme has begun, but there is plenty of the old Burnley left to remind us of its industrial heritage as a Lancashire cotton town. Familiar rows of terraced housing dominate the background. The mill chimneys are not there in the profusion of former years, but enough are left to evoke the memory of smoke darkened skies over Burnley. To the right, the Leeds to Liverpool Canal complements the industrial scene. If all this speaks of toil and the past, the area around Keirby Roundabout seemed, in 1962, to suggest a future of more leisure and pleasure. The Keirby Hotel, to the left, had opened in 1959 as a forward looking concept of Massey's Burnley Brewery. The Odeon Cinema, its sign clearly visible, was built in luxury mode, with expansive foyer, first floor lounge etc. The Mecca Locarno Ballroom can be seen, bottom right and the whole area suggests a 'mecca' of entertainment. Just as the leisure future never quite materialised, with British people working longer hours now than workers of any other country in the EEC, so the dreams of the leisure 'moguls' had mixed fortunes. The Keirby Hotel survives, albeit under a succession of different owners and names after the Massey Brewery closed down. The Locarno tried its hand at changing its name, becoming the 'Cat's Whiskers'. Later it became the 'Ritzy' night club, before closure. The Odeon was demolished in 1974 and perhaps significantly, the site is now occupied by Sainsburys. Maybe the great entertainment of now and the future is, 'Shop til you drop!'

On the move

Below: Tram No 54 for Towneley has literally come to the end of the line and is departing in the other direction in this shot taken in September 1926. Work was well advanced in building the New Culvert to carry the Leeds and Liverpool Canal over Yorkshire Street. The Old Culvert was a low and narrow affair, with two small arches at either side for pedestrians. How well the New Culvert looks in this photograph, with its shining new stone and its handsome carvings and decorative work.

Trams may now bring back fond memories and sighs of recollection, but in 1926 they were a modern form of transport. The Burnley and District Tram Company, founded in 1883, at first ran steam trams in Burnley and that must have been a sight to behold. By 1901 the Corporation had taken over the Company and the system was electrified the same year.

Trams had it all their own way for some years, but in 1924 the first motor buses were introduced to Burnley. Trams could not compete with this development and in 1935 the last one ran. The sound of the humming, clattering tram was gone, to be replaced by the snort and roar of the petrol engine. The tram had its romance; perhaps too the burning brazier and gas lamps in the photograph. But those who have had a cycle wheel stuck, or gone into a wobble on a motorbike, will tell you that there was not much romance in tramlines.

Right: The camera brings a worm's eye view of the new tram tracks being laid at Aqueduct Junction, Yorkshire Street, during the Culvert scheme of 1926 to 1927. Meanwhile the 'navvies' watch with interest the contortions that must have taken place to get this shot. At least there was no danger from behind, as the sign proclaims that the road was closed for 'vehicular traffic'. This can be read in spite of the jacket carelessly tossed over the sign, but it is unlikely that a road closure in 1926 would have caused just as much disruption in the town centre as it does today. The Culvert at the heart of the scheme was, in fact, the aqueduct which carries the Leeds and Liverpool Canal over Yorkshire Street and it involved some demolition, road widening and new tram rails. It must have caused tremendous local interest and although only one or two onlookers are captured in this photograph, other shots of this scheme show little knots of onlookers on all sides. Whatever happened to the noble pastime of watching men dig holes? Up to relatively recently, one or more men at work with a pick and shovel was sure to attract a cluster of Compo and Cleggy types, offering advice or simply 'chewing the fat'. The answer must surely be that nowadays, for every two workmen on a site, there seems to be one machine. Words of wisdom are drowned by the noise of diggers, not to mention the danger. The wiseacres have gone elsewhere, for road digging is not the spectator sport it used to be.

The residents of 49 Rosegrove Lane must have become accustomed to the sound of engines shunting wagons almost on their doorstep, but what they did not expect to find was one of the trucks across their doorstep. This dramatic photograph shows the scene the morning after the night before. At 2.50am, August 10th 1926, a coupling had broken between two wagons in the Rosegrove shunting yards. Thirty to forty wagons ran away, in spite of a railway worker trying to use his shunting pole as a brake. Reaching a speed of 40mph after 100 yards, the runaways fortunately hit four stationary wagons, which checked them. However, the four wagons were forced through the buffers, then a stone wall. They ploughed across Rosegrove Lane and one of them did severe damage to Mr Thomas Eastham's house, no 49. Another wagon brought a tram standard down, causing live wires to sprawl across the setts and tramlines. Incredibly, nobody was hurt, although Mr Eastham's two daughters, Lucy and Elsie, were treated for shock. The picture shows the busy scene later that morning and the Newton Heath breakdown gang had the debris cleared up by 11am. The wagon on the left looks as if it may have suffered the impact from the runaways and it is interesting to speculate as to what the man with the hook is trying to do. A crowd of onlookers has assembled in the background and it is a fair bet that the man on the wall at top left, wearing a trilby hat, is a news reporter.

Burnley Express

Burnley Express

Right: All the older forms of transport can be regarded with a degree of nostalgia, but just as with their modern equivalents they could go wrong, sometimes with fatal consequences. This horrifying scene from 1923 resulted from a runaway tram and considering the mass of twisted debris littering the ground, it is a wonder that only two were killed. At 12.10pm, on 22nd December 1923, a wagon which skidded on the snow hit tramcar No 10, on the Burnley to Harle Syke run. The impact forced the tram backwards and damaged its brakes, so that it ran out of control down a 300 yard long incline. The conductor emerges as a hero, for he threw two schoolchildren off the lower deck of the tram and they were both more-or-less unhurt, whilst another child jumped for it. At the sharp corner at Lanehead, the tram derailed and hit a shop and house. This literally severed the top deck from the bottom deck and the latter went on to plough through a garden wall. The conductor, who stuck to his post to the end, was killed, as was a 14 year old schoolgirl on the top deck. The driver, plus four other passengers, were hospitalised. The photograph speaks for itself, as grim faced people survey the wreckage. Christmas 1923 must have been a sad one in at least two households and the girl was an only child. Odd coincidences often emerge from disasters. The runaway tramcar flattened a pillar box which had only just been put in place to replace one damaged by a skidding wagon the previous week.

Below: A bold line in advertising, with no punches pulled, is the main theme of this photograph from the 1950s. The setting is the corner of Yorkshire Street and Belvedere Road. Advertising the function of a building, along with its wares, by large-scale lettering on the structure itself, seems now to be a thing of the past. 'Ham and Egg Teas' was the mouth-watering message that could sometimes be seen on roofs or gable ends out in the countryside.

It all suggested a kind of certainty; that things were going to remain the way they were for the foreseeable future. Nowadays, the function of a building can change so quickly - today a bank, tomorrow an insurance firm. It seems safer to hang up a sign, or a few detachable letters. In fact, the Rose and Thistle is hedging its bets a little bit. In spite of proclaiming that Dutton's is 'the best drink in town', a little sign advertising the Keighley brew of Taylor's has been sneaked in over the club door, presumably for those who don't mind second-best. Whatever the drink, the Rose and Thistle was close enough to Turf Moor for the match regulars to conduct their football previews or 'post-mortems' there. The garage too displays some familiar advertising names in those of Cleveland and Dunlop. This was long before the days of self-service and you were likely to have your tank filled by someone who had just come out from beneath a motor. You would have got some funny looks if you had asked for some crisps and chocolate as well.

'Blackpool here we come', might well be the caption for this photograph which, judging by ladies' hats, seems to belong to the 1930s. The scene is the old bus station at Parker Lane and a queue of people ready to get away from it all. Going away for an annual holiday came within the reach of more and more people between the wars and whereas it was the nineteen century growth of railways that caused the boom in seaside resorts, the charabanc was offering an alternative mode of transport by the 1930s. People often had little choice in the timing of their Summer holidays. Each Northern mill town and city virtually closed down during its own 'Wakes Weeks', Burnley's traditionally falling during the first two weeks in July. After World War Two, with increased

prosperity, towns like Burnley could appear almost to be 'ghost' towns during 'Wakes', as the annual exodus took place. You could always bump into lots of pals in Blackpool and some people went to the same boarding house, year in year out. Memories of old-style boarding houses could fill a book - meals 'on the dot'; baths by appointment only; out of the house by 9.30am and no

return until 12 noon, even if a typhoon was sweeping the promenade. How things have changed since the competition arose from cheap package holidays abroad. The destinations now are much more exotic, partly because of the unpredictability of the British weather. Speaking of which, it seems a very good idea to have a shop called Waterproofs next to a holiday bus station.

Above: For those who endured it, the infamous Winter of early 1947 will be for ever deeply etched in their memories. This photograph of a wagon armed with snowplough, trying to clear a path through snowdrifts for the traffic behind, gives just a flavour of that time. The fact also that this scene, near the Waggoners' Inn in Manchester Road, was captured in March, gives some idea of the wearisome length of that Winter.

The crocus and daffodil were definitely late that year. Coming at it did, only two years after the end of a gruelling war and with rationing and fuel shortages still a fact of life, misery was widespread. For over two months, from January 1947, Britain froze up and Burnley was no exception. Coal was desperately short and local firms who sold wooden logs were inundated with orders. By early February, parts of the Leeds and Liverpool Canal had frozen and by mid-February coal barges were marooned at Hapton and Nelson. Ice-breakers were helpless against a solid glacial mass. This meant that power generating stations were starved of coal and power cuts were increased.

Milk came frozen on the step, as did even eggs. One poor Burnley housewife was trapped in her house because both front and back doors had swollen and frozen. On the hills around Burnley, farms were cut off by huge drifts and hundreds of sheep were lost. The children made the most of it, but even they were not sorry when Winter finally began to relax its grip in late March.

Right: The 'highway in the sky' was the name given to Burnley's £800,000 Centenary Way when it opened in June 1967 and indeed from this perspective it does seem to fly over the valley towards the distant roundabout. Work is nearing completion here, prior to the grand opening on June 11th 1967. The Centenary referred to was the 100th Anniversary of Burnley's incorporation as a chartered borough, which had been celebrated in 1961. At this time also, a scheme was already underway to build ring roads in order to ease traffic congestion in the town centre. Centenary Way was not quite the completion of the system, but the amount of work that had been done can be gauged from the fact that total expenditure on highways had been £2,300,000 since 1952. The opening ceremony was a stylish affair, in which Alderman H Hudson turned an electronic key which triggered off a three foot length of cordite. The ensuing minor explosion removed the velvet drape covering a commemorative stone near the Manchester Road and Trafalgar Street roundabout. A more traditional ribbon cutting ceremony at the junction of Centenary Way and Grimshaw Street allowed a 14 car calvacade to proceed up the new stretch of road, headed by the car containing the Mayor and Mayoress, Alderman and Mrs J H Sutcliffe. If Centenary Way pointed the way to the future, it skirted some symbols of the past as it headed across its giant concrete pillars, none more so than the Tripe Works to the left of the photograph. The time was well past when tripe, cowheel and elder formed a major part of the diet of working-class households.

Shopping spree

Left: This interesting scene of the interior of the old Market Hall was captured around the 1890s. It may well have been 1897, for the flags which hang from the roof suggest a celebration and 1897 marked the Diamond Jubilee of Queen Victoria. This grand old lady had occupied the throne for the previous 60 years, a span of time which had seen Britain grow to industrial pre-eminence in the World. Along with industrial power had come military power and Britain possessed a huge fleet with which to protect the largest empire ever seen. Imperial glory was the theme of the Diamond Jubilee, but no matter how patriotic the two ladies in the foreground felt, they were probably discussing more mundane matters pertaining to crockery. John Harrison's dinner service for six people, at ten shillings and six pence (521/2p), looks an absolute bargain, but we must remember that it was not uncommon for an adult male labourer to earn only £1 per week at that time. The two ladies are dressed in that mixture of the forbidding and the charming which seemed to be a hallmark of the fashions of the day. The one on the right, for example, presents a typically severe Victorian image in the shape of her long, dark dress and high buttoned neck, but manages to soften the effect by sporting a pleasant straw boater on top. The headgear of the lady on the left is equally fascinating, perhaps part of the stallholder's uniform. And what about that crockery, piled high in such a precarious fashion? It appears as if one nudge from the slightly camera-shy young man in the rear would bring the whole lot crashing down.

Above: and below: These two fascinating window displays from the Co-operative Stores on Hammerton Street offer a complete contrast in advertising styles. The rolls, bales and piles of cloth in one of them, all with various prices attached, convey a practical, no-nonsense attitude. The CWS signpost indicates, 'The Better Way' and it is as simple as that. 'Come and see for yourself; we have nothing to hide', seems to be the message. The labels indicate 'bleached', 'cotton', 'all wool' and 'flannel', not a shred of nylon or rayon in sight. And, as befits a Burnley store, the dominant theme is cotton. This suggests an inter-war period, when cotton was still 'king' in Lancashire in general and in Burnley in particular. Markets had been lost during the First World War and foreign competition was fierce, but it was not until after the Second World War that man-made fibres began to make a severe impact on the industry. The second window display is, admittedly, advertising a much more glamorous product, but the approach is much more imaginative in its exploitation of the world of entertainment. The beautiful wedding gowns on display are endorsed by that most glamorous star of the film world, Mae West. There she is at the rear, to the right of the church entrance, in itself a reminder that it was most unusual for a wedding to be held anywhere else in those days. No doubt the Palace Theatre was glad enough to have its current film, 'I'm No Angel', starring Mae West, advertised in the window of the local Co-operative Store - a nice bit of mutual co-operation here. Stills from the film also feature prominently at the front of the window and the evidence of the fashion and the film seems to place this display in the 1930s. The nicest touch of all may be seen on the far left. Many readers will know Miss West's famous catch phrase - the more respectable one - 'Come up and see me sometime'. Beneath the words 'Wedding Trousseau' may be seen the Co-op's own version of this - 'Come in and see us sometime'.

Burnley Express

The Burnley town centre redevelopment plan of the 1960s inevitably meant the loss of impressive old buildings which, to some people, must have felt like having the very heart of the town torn out. The old Market Hall was surely one of these buildings and the hoardings around the building on this picture indicate that demolition was nigh. Burnley first received a charter to hold a weekly market in 1294, granted to Henry de Lacy by Edward I. The old market place was near the parish church at Top o' th' Town and one can imagine the busy trade in livestock and agricultural produce, along with craft products. In 1829 the Burnley Market Company built a Market Hall, but the building which is the subject of the photograph was not constructed until 1870. And what a fine and spacious building it was, with its classical frontage and arches. The main entrance looks very well, with its distinctive pillars and wrought iron work. However how much grander the whole edifice must have looked in 1870, with its new

and glistening stonework, before nearly a century of industrial soot and smoke began to blacken its features. Progress marches on and in 1966 the Victorian Market Hall was demolished. On the negative side was the fact that the building which replaced it was very plain and functional. On the positive side was the opening out of the area to pedestrianisation and the pleasures of traffic-free shopping.

Whatever the 'pros' and 'cons', a demolition usually makes a sad sight and in this photograph there seems to be little left of the old Market Hall other than the once proud entry from Chancery Street. The last of the bargaining and bartering was over for this particular building - not even a packet of Clampett's All-One Day Meal to be had in spite of the forlorn poster in the foreground. The picture evokes the sounds of crashing masonry and clouds of dust blowing around the market square, as Burnley town centre passed from one era to the next.

What a different prospect the camera would see now, almost 40 years on, from the one featured here, which was so familiar in 1960. The old Market Hall just comes into view on the right with the canvas awnings of the market traders spreading across the old Market Square. The metal frameworks to the right suggest that there is room for more, so in spite of the presence of lots of vehicles, it is probably still quite early in the day. We are looking down Market Street, with Howe Street at the top and if sounds are as evocative as views, then the memory of the rumble of a wagon down setts should add an extra dimension to this photograph. The public house sign high up to the left is that of the New Market Hotel, a Massey House, very handily placed to cater to the needs of market traders and customers. There was, however, plenty of competition in the immediate vicinity. Altham's Walk-Round Store would have kept its prices pretty 'keen', being so close to the market and it is now a name with totally different business connotations. What the lady and gentleman are discussing at the rear of the van we will never know, but as this was the market area, it might literally have been 'the price of nails'. The 1960s central area re-development scheme changed this prospect entirely. The demolition of the old Market Hall, with all the associated regrets, was to begin only six years after this photograph was taken.

Burnley Express

Left: A new phase in the war against crime began in 1952, as the foundation stone for the new law courts and police station was laid on the site of the old cattle market. The scheme was to take three years to complete and marks an early phase in a succession of changes that have transformed the centre of Burnley. For example, the opening of the Keirby Hotel was to follow in 1959 and the new bus station in 1964. An interested crowd of onlookers has gathered around the safety barrier in our photograph of what appears to be a rather grey day in 1952. The headgear is very much of the day, for in 1952 flat caps and headscarves could put in an appearance even on formal occasions. Not that the formality has yet begun, for there is no sign of the dignitaries who always accompany such occasions. In fact, mothers strolling by with their children and a lady walking her dog, are the only sign of activity. The hoardings around the site do not quite hide a view of Burnley

that was soon to change so radically. Even the largest projects have to start somewhere and few of the spectators could have visualised the building that would be created from two holes in the setts. However, arise it did and at the opening of the new courts and police station in 1955, Burnley's Recorder, Mr N J Laski QC, was to comment that the building was much more suitable for the administration of justice than the Town Hall, even though he had happy memories of the latter.

Above: This photograph shows the old market interior, but this time in 1965, shortly before demolition. Fashions have certainly changed, but what is most impressive is not the change, but the continuity. Almost 70 years on and the name of Harrison is still selling crockery, a fine tradition. It has to be said, however, that the wares have not been piled up with the same abandon as in the 1897 shot.

At work

A great amount of work was going on between 1926 and 1927 on the Culvert, which carries the Leeds and Liverpool Canal across Yorkshire Street. The contractors were Wellerman Bros of Sheffield and Hyde, as the photograph shows and it has to be said that a splendid job has been made, despite the Yorkshire and Cheshire origins of the firm. Not only that, the imposing frontage of the Yorkshire Hotel forms a backdrop. How could Lancastrians bear to spend so much money in a hotel of that name and give it such a prosperous look? Clearly the road has been widened, otherwise the old gas lamps would not be in such a preposterous position, seemingly in the middle of the road. The scaffolding on the right seems to indicate some property demolition also. The next step would be the laying of tram tracks. Not a lot seems to be going on at this end, in spite of an untidy spread of picks, shovels and the like. The activity is all concentrated at the far end, near the Yorkshire Hotel.

The photographer has obviously progressed on to this hive of activity and has captured a huge number of men at work.

This term is used loosely, for they are very much aware of the camera and have paused in their work. It would have been virtually impossible to take an informal snapshot in those days, with the amount of equipment to be carted around and set up. The working dress is very much of the 1920s, with jackets off and sleeves rolled up. Waistcoats and flat hats were, of course, obligatory. Although the picture is dated September 1926, even had it been 'flaming June', it is doubtful whether they would have gone much further in 'doffing off', certainly not as far as their near naked modern counterparts. Another difference from today is the actual number of workers on the site. 'Navvying' was very labour intensive, all pick, shovel and wheelbarrow. There is not a piece of machinery in sight. The night watchman's hut is there and this too seems to belong to the past now, along with the glow of the burning brazier outside the hut at night.

The never-ending roadworks of today usually bring complaints about loss of trade from local businesses. One cannot imagine the Yorkshire Hotel complaining about a host of thirsty workmen outside its door.

With a traditional cutting of the tape the Mayor of Burnley, Councillor James Sutcliffe, opens the New Culvert in 1927, while other local worthies and members of the constabulary look on. The work on this scheme, which centred on the canal aqueduct over Yorkshire Street and associated road improvements, went on from 1926 to 1927. It was considered important enough to warrant such a distinguished gathering to launch the New Culvert. Although the contractors were Wellerman Bros from Sheffield and Hyde, it is likely that they employed a lot of local labour on the scheme. This was important in the 1920s, generally years of depression. In 1918, at the end of the Great War, Lloyd George had promised 'homes fit for heroes', but the men of Burnley and elsewhere, had returned to find textiles jobs disappearing. 'King Cotton' appeared to be fighting a losing battle as markets lost during the war were never recovered. In the year the New Culvert scheme began, 1926, resentment came to a head in the General Strike. Therefore, corporation sponsored schemes not only improved the town, but provided much needed employment. Certainly the Mayor and his fellow dignitaries seem to display a quiet pride as they gaze down at the shining new setts and tramlines.

'Eyes front' for the Burnley Police Force under inspection in 1938 and what a fine body of men they are, from the toes of their shining shoes to the gleaming tips of their helmets. The sergeant, nearest to the camera, has his service medals proudly on display, so this must have been something of a special occasion in what appears to be a gymnasium. By 1938 the police force had come a long way since the days of the frock-coated and top-hatted 'Peelers' or 'Bobbies' of the 1840s, nicknamed after the Prime Minister of the day and a man with Lancashire roots, Sir Robert Peel. Perhaps Burnley was a particularly law-abiding place, or perhaps it was to do with cost, but the borough seemed reluctant to form its own police force until compelled to do so by law in 1887. Until that date, outside authorities controlled the policing of Burnley. This first force consisted of a Chief Constable, three inspectors, six sergeants and sixty constables. The force was based at the Town Hall, which was built in 1888 and which also housed the Burnley Magistrates Court. From 1955, both the police force and law courts were centred in the new building erected on the site of the old cattle market. Our 1938 photograph shows some sort of truncheon inspection and the constables hold their hands in regulation position for the display of their truncheons. Just what exactly is being inspected is an intriguing question, but the man in charge has some sort of small instrument in his hand. In 1938, of course, the most familiar sighting of these 'bobbies' would be 'on the beat', rather than in police cars.

Burnley Express

Above: This view from the dock of the Burnley Bench of Magistrates in 1938 would surely have deterred petty criminals from any further offences if the magistrates had ever decided to all sit together. The Chairman of the Bench, with his chain of office, sits in the very finely carved chair in the middle, with the court usher to the left of the chair and his fellow magistrates on both sides. Policemen and officials sit below, including the very important clerk to the court. The Burnley Magistrates Court dates from 1872 and the right to deal with more serious crimes, in Quarter Sessions, was granted in 1893. The Town Hall was the court's base until 1955, when the administration of justice was moved to a new building built on the site of the old cattle market. This new building also became the new Police Headquarters. The interior of the Town Hall court, shown in the photograph, is typical of its day, with polished panelling and benches, along with quilted leather backed seats. The hexagonal witness box stands on the left. The business of a magistrate is a serious one and those who undertake its duties carry a heavy responsibility, but no doubt the court had its lighter moments. Every aspect of Burnley life, from the tragic to the comic, must have been on display in this court over the course of the years. As one famous newspaper once said, 'All life is here'.

Right: This view of Halstead's Forge or Blacksmith's Shop, in Yorkshire Street, was a subject for nostalgia even in 1930. To the obvious regret of many, the old premises were about to be converted to a tripe shop. The forge had been established in 1830 by Mr Halstead Halstead and one century later it was in the hands of his grandson, Walter Halstead. The picture is a reminder of how important horses were to trade and industry at one time, for in its heyday the forge had employed as many as eight smiths. A roaring trade was done shoeing the 'lime gals', the little pack ponies which carried lime to farmers across the Pennines. Also, 160 horses of the Burnley Carriage Company were regularly shod at Halstead's. Many were the stories that the smiths could tell, for example about the obstinate mule, 'Kicking Sarah', who apparently kicked one smith right across the street. Or then there was the tale of the eloping couple who believed that Gretna Green was in Burnley and that the famous marriage anvil was at Halstead's. The leather aprons and clogs are evocative enough, but what the photograph cannot capture is the sizzle as the hot shoe went in the water, or the acrid smell of the steam and smoke. Halstead's Forge was transferring to Blakey Street in 1930 and it was a sign of the changing times that it was combining with a wheelwright and motor builders

These two shots take in the old Manchester Road Fire Station, around 1960, before operations were transferred to the new station on Belvedere Road in 1965. The two fire engines fit very snugly, not to say tightly, in their garages, whilst the firemen stand ready at the doors. With the engines out on the street, a closer look is afforded of these powerful vehicles, particularly the 'Dennis' at the front. All the necessary paraphernalia is there to be seen - lights, bells, klaxon horn and extending ladders. Fire fighting in Burnley seems to have been a rather haphazard affair in the middle of the nineteenth century. While the fire raged, the fire chief's first concern was to see that those in need of help could pay for it, or were insured against fire. In 1873, the Corporation could only boast two old horse-drawn hand engines, but a steam engine with four jets was purchased in 1874, at a cost of £1,444. One wonders how this rudimentary equipment coped with the huge mill fires that occasionally occurred in Burnley. The fire station itself was on Manchester Road, although the one featured in the pictures was not built until 1881, on the site of the old one, at a cost of £1,250. Fire fighting has come a long way since the days of the horse clip-clopping over the setts of Burnley, pulling some primitive machine behind it. Early photographs show very little in the way of safety equipment, not even helmets. How those pioneers would have looked with amazement at such advances as breathing apparatus, 'walkie talkie' radios and the rest. In fact, most of these are of relatively recent origin and you need not be so old as to remember hearing the siren go to warn the firemen to get down to the station. Whatever the century, firemen old and new have always done essentially the same job and a dangerous one at that.

Burnley Express

Burnley Express

'Here we go. Here we go. Here we go'. This might be the title theme of this view of the building of the Keirby Roundabout in 1961, the first phase of the re-development plan of the 1960s. Towns are constantly changing and in the great wave of welfare reform that followed the Second World War, Burnley Corporation built 4,500 council houses, on 14 surrounding estates, between 1945 and 1960. By the latter date, however, the focus was the town centre and how best to modernise it in order both to attract retailers and make life more pleasant for the shoppers. This required not so much change as radical transfor-mation, as the town centre was cleared to create traffic-free zones, shopping malls, ring roads and car parks. A landmark in this process was the demolition of the old Market Hall in 1966. Modernisation comes at a price and what some counted as a gain in terms of a cleaner, brighter town centre, others saw as a loss in terms of the demise of some fine old buildings. The Keirby Hotel, opened in 1959 and dominating the centre of the picture, seemed to symbolise the changes to come. Its architecture was 'modern', a word which could be uttered in praise or damnation, according to one's point of view. The Keirby was the luxury flagship hotel of Massey's Burnley Brewery and was named after a former brewery on the site. After Massey's closure, the Keirby has taken on many new identities, but it is at present the Comfort Friendly Stop Inn. The lesson of change is, of course, that its prophets eventually became its victims. The Odeon, to the right, was built as a luxury, modernistic cinema of the new age, but had been demolished by 1974.